Through It All

by Genevieve Taylor

THROUGH IT ALL
By Genevieve Taylor

© 2007 by Genevieve Taylor

ISBN# 1-897373-13-9

All scripture quotations are taken from the HOLY BIBLE, NEW INTERNATIONAL VERSION®. NIV®. Copyright ©1973, 1978, 1984 by International Bible Society. Used by permission of Zondervan. All rights reserved.

Song lyrics quoted have been used by permission. (See the References page for details.)

WORD ALIVE PRESS

Printed by Word Alive Press
131 Cordite Road, Winnipeg, MB R3W 1S1
www.wordalivepress.ca

Through It All is dedicated to those who are, have and will walk through tough circumstances to come out shining more radiant. This is to be a voice for those who feel afraid to speak up due to concern that they might be misunderstood. You are worth it!

Preface

THERE IS NO WAY I could complete my story without excerpts from those who have and will continue to surround me. None of us walks alone, and everyone's piece of the puzzle (written here in their own words) has helped to vividly capture and create a bigger picture, especially in light of my memories that are misplaced.

While it might not make sense now as you glance through the pages, in the end you should be able to comprehend and begin to fully understand the journey that God has taken me on.

My prayer is that the words will come alive and bounce off the pages right into your heart to bring you enlightenment as you walk through and pen your own life's story.

~Genevieve

THROUGH IT ALL
Table of Contents

A Letter from Derek

MAY 29TH, 2005…WHAT A DAY! I have had some special days in my life, like the day I married my best friend Genevieve, but this one was even more unique. This was the day that Genevieve and I met and held our new baby for the first time as we welcomed her into this world. We had carried on many discussions with her, and I had even given many hugs and kisses before this day, but finally this was the day I could put a face to the beautiful baby girl who had been so safely protected within Genevieve.

Her name was Hope. From the day we started talking about having children, we both felt in our hearts that if we had a baby girl, without question, her name would be Hope. Little did we know at that time, many years ago, how significant she and her name would be through the journey that we were about to embark on.

What I am about to tell you is likely one of the hardest things I've ever had to write about to date, because it refers to a time for me that is probably best left in the past. Having said this, I feel it's the least I can do in support of Genevieve, because what she has gone through, fully recovered from, and is now writing about is far more heroic than what I'm about to say, and I'm truly honored to have this opportunity to show how strong and special of a person Genevieve is to her family and friends as well as to Hope and I.

I know this book will change your life forever—there's no way it won't—for it will prove and confirm that you never know how important someone is in your life until they are (or are almost) taken from you. I am blessed that I was spared losing Genevieve, and not a day goes by that I don't thank God for her and Hope. My girls are my life. They mean everything to me and I certainly couldn't imagine life any other way today without them. When you become a father, you see life in an entirely different way. I don't mean good or bad, just different.

I had no idea it was even remotely possible to experience two consecutive life-changing events on such opposite spectrums of emotion. What I mean is, here Genevieve and I were, the newly proud parents of a healthy baby girl, when such disaster struck that I went from being on top of the world to being well below the world in a few very short days.

Within two weeks of Hope's birth, Genevieve was diagnosed with postpartum psychosis.

My job takes me all over the world. What I find truly mesmerizing is that I can be sipping on a cappuccino in Paris, France, or looking at the beautiful ships in the downtown harbor in Sydney, Australia, in the morning, and be back at home sitting on my deck in the evening enjoying the company of Genevieve and Hope all in the same day. I find myself asking the question, *how is this possible?* It is truly amazing. It's also the only way I can think to describe how I felt when I learned about what Genevieve was experiencing with her illness. A perfect world, a perfect family, were all changed in mere hours. *How was this possible?*

Now that I look back and remember the days leading up to Genevieve's sickness, I can see it all unfold, and I realize it happened right before my eyes. See, I remember being part of all the prenatal classes, and don't get me wrong, they were enormously helpful and the health region staff did a fantastic job. But the one thing they didn't teach us in the prenatal classes was how to determine if your wife is experiencing postpartum psychosis. The classes touch on postpartum depression, better known as the "Baby Blues," but not on postpartum psychosis—and who can blame them? I wouldn't have been particularly excited to find out that there was the potential for my wife to become very ill following what could possibly be the best day of our lives, giving birth to our new child. After all, postpartum psychosis is as rare as 1 in 1000 according to statistics, so why scare an entire class of soon-to-be parents with such a rare illness? Well, we were the unfortunate 1 in 1000 to go through this trial that turned our world upside down, leaving me asking the question, "Why, Lord, of all the people in this world, why us?"

If you are not familiar with the term *postpartum psychosis*, it is a condition often described as the contributing factor in a woman taking her baby's life, her own life or, in some cases, maybe both. I'm so very thankful this wasn't the case for my family!

I remember coming downstairs one Sunday morning two weeks following Hope's arrival to Genevieve greeting me by saying, "Derek, something is just not right with me and I need to call the Early Start help line." I agreed, and this began a journey over the next several months that I had no idea would be so difficult. I was told to take Genevieve to the emergency room at the Rockyview General Hospital in Calgary, which specialized in postpartum psychosis. The first of many very hard and gut-wrenching decisions that would have to be made throughout this journey was made that Sunday evening; I had to agree to admit my wife—my best friend and the mother of my child—to a psychiatric ward, which you will better come to know throughout Genevieve's book as "Unit 49."

I remember that night like it was last night. I walked beside Genevieve as a security guard and a nurse wheeled her in a wheelchair from the emergency room to Unit 49. I fought back the tears, trying to be strong for my wife and at the same time trying to convince her (and myself) that locking her up in the hospital was for her own good. This could simply have been one of, if not *the* hardest decisions

I've made in life, as Genevieve continued to ask me why I was doing this to her by admitting her into the hospital. All I could think about was that she was ill in her mind and didn't really mean what she was saying to me. I had never been to a psychiatric ward prior to this, but it was pretty much what I had prepared myself for.

I helped her settle in for the night and at midnight was asked to say good-bye. I have always thought of how hard it will be to say good-bye to Hope when she goes to school for that first day (as this will surely show that she is growing up), but saying good-bye to my wife, who was to be locked up in the hospital for who knows how long, had to be exponentially harder.

I think that the glass windows in the doors that separate Unit 49 from the rest of the hospital are completely inappropriate. I found it very ironic that I had admitted my wife to the hospital to get better, but all she could see was me walking *away* from her as I walked down the long hallway to the parking garage (that I would soon purchase a monthly pass to park at). I remember walking down the hallway saying to myself, "Okay. When I look back I hope she is not still watching me walk away." Unfortunately, she would watch me the entire way until I turned to go out the doors, waving good-bye with a sad face that I hope to never see again. As days passed, it became much easier for me to convince her to let me tuck her in for the night and kiss her goodnight before I left, because then I would know she wouldn't be watching me walk down that hallway to the parking garage that seemed to go on for miles. I felt so bad that I was able to go home to Hope, while Genevieve had to stay at the hospital missing out on all the "firsts" that Hope would do.

During this very difficult and exhausting time, I was so very blessed that Hope slept through the night very early in her life—literally a few weeks after being born. This gave me the much-needed time to rest, so that I could try to be the very best husband I could be to the wife I so very much missed having at home sharing these special times with Hope. I think what was the hardest to grasp was the fact that it was a great possibility that Genevieve would never have the chance to experience the things a mother deserved the right to experience, because the doctors now recommended that we not have any more children. We had always planned for at least two, so this was not an easy thing to hear from the doctors. I guess this is why my heart ached at the fact that I was able to experience Hope just being born, but Genevieve wasn't able to.

The Genevieve I had known a week prior—the one that I was celebrating the arrival of our new daughter with—was simply not the Genevieve I found in the hospital. Remember how I said how quickly things changed from our journey of parenthood to our journey of Genevieve surviving this illness of postpartum psychosis? Well, it became far worse when I realized Genevieve didn't think she had a daughter, and even more, didn't even know we were married to each other. I couldn't believe what I was hearing. To put it very bluntly, my wife had completely lost her mind. She was entirely on another planet. I don't say these things to be rude or mean; this was the sheer truth, and I didn't know this lady, because she simply didn't know me, her husband, or her daughter, Hope. I'm thankful this didn't last longer than a week, as I'm sure you can only imagine the impact of this type of situation. Having someone you love more than life itself left only with you in body—absent from mind and soul—is not an easy reality to go home to at night and try to reason with.

Three weeks had passed in the hospital and Genevieve had shown huge improvement. So much improvement, in fact, that the doctor said she was able to go home, and I can remember us as a family rejoicing that we could start all over again and do the best we could to forget about what had just happened. At least, we would try to forget about it as best we could, given the ongoing medication that Genevieve was told she would have to take for the rest of her life. It seemed like a small price to pay for where she was a few weeks before compared with where she was that glorious day she was released.

Everything was going great the following week after she was discharged, that is, until the fifth day she was out, when she unfortunately took a turn for the worse. Genevieve had a relapse, and I can't begin to describe how completely this took the wind out of our sails. We found ourselves back with the doctor later that week, only to hear from the doctor that Genevieve was going to have to be re-admitted and that they were going to be much more cautious about letting her out this time. The only translation I could take from this news was that she was going to have to go back to Unit 49 for a much longer time until they were confident that she was healed.

I still laugh as I recall a remark Genevieve made while I was walking her back to Unit 49 for the second time to be re-admitted. She said, "If only I had smiled more to the doctor, they wouldn't have made me come back here this time." I know it wasn't very funny under the circumstances, but it brought back memories of her telling me how she once avoided a speeding ticket by smiling to the police officer. I still smile to think that Genevieve thought this might have worked on the doctor in this situation too.

I remember selfishly thinking to myself, "How will I continue to pull all of this off—making one trip to the hospital in the afternoon so she can hold Hope to ensure that Hope knows who her mother is, a second trip to the hospital in the evening to provide the much required support she requires each day while at the same time maintaining my full-time job?" I guess the Lord gave me supernatural strength to hold it together for five more weeks. My family and friends also helped me get through this very difficult time in my life, and I'm not sure how Hope and I would have made it without them all helping out when and where required.

Following two full months in Unit 49, once again Genevieve was released from the hospital. One of the things that I was so proud of Genevieve for was that she accepted the treatment while in the hospital. Another thing was that she was so nice to her fellow patients. She would always say hi to them and introduce me to them like they were her long lost friends. That's just the way Genevieve is. The nurses also got to know me pretty well around there because of the time I spent there visiting, and every single one of them would always say how beautiful my wife's voice was. They would say, "She has a voice like an Angel," to which I would reply, "I know! I sure miss that about not having her at home." For some reason Hope just wouldn't calm when I sang to her like she would when Genevieve sang to her…I can't understand why, though.

I'm thrilled to write that Genevieve is at 110% today, completely healed and the best wife and mother I know. I have always been so proud of her— from the day I met her when we were young teenagers throughout the journey to the mighty woman of God she has become today. She continues to amaze me with her ambition and her willingness to share with the world that her life is a miracle. You see, when she was admitted to Unit 49, the doctors made it clear to me that she would certainly have to take medication for the remainder of her life, and that some sort of depression or bipolar disorder was very likely going to be part of her natural future. I don't have to tell you that under my breath I said, "I do not believe and accept that; my wife will be fully healed in Jesus' name."

One thing I find so very encouraging is that through it all Genevieve is not ashamed of what she has conquered, and neither are Hope or I ashamed of it either. Postpartum psychosis is a mental illness like any other illness—one that can be beaten against all odds. It goes without saying that I spent many hours in prayer, and I truly believe our faith helped us persevere "Through It All."

Hope and I love you, Genevieve, and we're so very proud to have you back home and in our lives forever. We are both eager to support you with your dreams, and as a family we feel we can make it through any path that is put before us.

Love Always,
~*Derek and Hope*

THROUGH IT ALL
Creating a Song

EVERYONE HAS A UNIQUE SONG to sing. Throughout our lives there may be melodies of joy mingled with songs of heartache, but in the midst there is always a tugging on our heart strings to search within and pull out that distinctive song that only we can sing. The tempo and tune will change, as well as the flavor and style, but one thing remains constant— this song is your own. No one can take your song away as you release the essence and beauty of capturing life.

Enjoy the moment, that's what they say, and now more than ever I grasp the true meaning. Life is a journey and you can never know or even imagine how it is going to play out.

I have always been a dreamer. But one day my dream bubble burst and I ended up in another world. I now belonged to a world where reality no longer existed. I never understood how I got to this place, yet I was always aware of a longing to get out. My dreams can't be blamed for getting me to that point; rather, it was caused by a mere chemical imbalance. Not even the professionals can fully explain why these imbalances occur. It wasn't that things were awful in my everyday life and I needed to escape—I couldn't have been happier with life. Actually, one the happiest moments that I can recall was as I held my baby for the first time with my loving husband right beside me.

How could everything come flooding in to choke the life out of the real me and turn me into someone I never knew existed? How could I not know who my new daughter was or even recognize my husband? How could this happen to me? These are memories lost that will never return. Strangely enough, though, I am not sure I want to remember.

Remember?

Oh yes, this is what I do remember…

☙ ❧

It is truly amazing when you receive your heart's desire. In the summer of 2004, I started to think about what it would be like to have a "little one." How different our life would be! Now, you have to understand something. Having children was never a real distinct possibility for me. My goals, ambitions and dreams all focused on becoming a career woman. I had the determination and the drive to accomplish this. I had all that I could want: my prince, my castle, my carriage and the most important thing to any princess—the walk in closet complete with a princess wardrobe.

But one day, while on a cruise, a "God feeling" occurred. I felt a sudden heart desire to have a baby. How could I wake up and change from being content to feeling that something or someone was missing in my life? I thought this fleeting emotion would go away, but it began to take deep root within my heart as my seed of longing sprouted. I shared my heart with my husband, and we both decided that it was the right time. Together our excitement and anticipation rose as we went on our journey of baby-making.

Even so, there was always a little thought of hesitation in my head. Children are amazing, but where in all my goals and plans would they fit? Being a career woman was on my agenda, and I would often tease my husband, Derek, that he would have to be Mr. Mom. Was I ready to exchange my designer suits—labeled "dry clean only"—for easy-to-wear, practical, machine-washable garments?

Women are always looking for a product to give them a radiant glow, the same glow that pregnant women have. Before I even knew I was pregnant, my colleagues and clients began to quietly ask me, "Are you not telling us something? You just seem to have this glow."

With my eyes lit up I replied, "I'll let you know. Something seems so different, but I have no idea, nor have I taken any tests." Tests? To say it seemed so final, but it was apparent I just needed to know.

On September 29, 2004, during a regular trip to the grocery store, I found myself going down an aisle that I normally ignore. I felt overwhelmed by the multitude of choices for this one simple test. I had never seriously considered that choosing a pregnancy test might be this complicated. When I arrived home all I could think about was, "Should I take the test now or wait until Derek arrives back from Austria?"

With much uncertainty, I figured I'd better call him on the other side of the world to help me make my decision. I proceeded to call, and although I woke him in the middle of the night, he gave me the go ahead to take the test.

The box claimed that within one minute it would have the clearest result. Not only was that the longest minute I have ever experienced, but the result didn't seem very clear at all. I was looking at a very dark vertical line crossed by a faint horizontal line. What did that mean? I looked on the box for more answers and found a 1-800 number to call with my questions. Immediately I had a lady on the line, and I explained all that occurred and that it appeared to have a "+" sign but the horizontal line was so faint compared to the vertical one. She assured me that it didn't matter, and that the vertical line is brighter than the horizontal, which means you are pregnant. Her accent was so thick, I wasn't sure I was hearing her right. I had her confirm everything very slowly to ensure I was hearing her correctly. "Congratulations!" she replied. I couldn't believe it. My heart leaped for joy.

It felt like a dream. I immediately called my husband back and awoke my Prince Charming with the news. "We are having a baby!" The time zone difference, coupled with me waking him up in the middle of the night, made it feel like only a dream, but soon the reality of it all began to sink in. He was so happy to think that this could happen to us right away.

I still remember how I felt that Saturday as I went to pick up the "daddy–to-be" at the airport. I felt so giddy as I waited for Derek to come off the plane. We were finally able to hold each other and celebrate the new little miracle of life that we so desired. As we turned the next page in the story of our love that continues to grow and change, we couldn't help but look at each other with a new sparkle in our eyes. Our love for each other, a love that had been just between two people, was now growing to include this little one who was so beautifully and intricately forming inside.

It is amazing what your body goes through during pregnancy. The metamorphosis is actually quite astounding. Let's just say I felt a little topsy-turvy, like on a carnival ride. One minute you are so excited to get on the ride, and then suddenly you feel a little queasy and you beg to get off this "tilt-a–whirl." Throughout the ever-changing emotions and body transformations, a few words from a song kept playing in my head, "It's gonna be worth it, it's gonna be worth it, it's gonna be worth it all."

"Worth It All"[1]
by Rita Springer

I don't understand Your ways

Oh but I will give You my song
Give You all of my praise
You hold on to all my pain
With it You are pulling me closer
And pulling me into Your ways

Now around every corner
And up every mountain
I'm not looking for crowns
Or the water from fountains
I'm desperate in seeking, frantic believing
That the sight of Your face
Is all that I need
I will say to You

It's gonna be worth it
It's gonna be worth it
It's gonna be worth it all
I believe this

You're gonna be worth it
You're gonna be worth it
You're gonna be worth it all
I believe this

It couldn't have been truer as we listened to our baby's heartbeat for the very first time. I'll never forget the moment, with tears glistening in our eyes, as we watched our baby's movements as she danced around the womb so free and full of life. She ended her first TV screen debut and photo session with a lasting impression of her sucking her thumb. It was after this that we started to understand why my body was so tired and why I was feeling this array of emotions. A baby was developing inside!

This was such a unique experience for me. One week I could wear my favorite skirt and then the next week somehow it had shrunk. While the expanding part of the pregnancy was fun, knowing that I had to experience that monthly pre-natal visit and its dreaded 'weigh in' was not something I enjoyed. I was always sure there was something wrong with the scale, but the nurses assured me all was well.

I remember my first pre-natal visit, where I became accustomed to the check-ups that would be my new monthly routine. The nurse had the biggest smile on her face as she called me into the room. She asked, "This is your first pregnancy?" She gazed at my outfit, which consisted of a cream-colored suit jacket trimmed with a faux fur collar, a unique pleated jean skirt and my black leather stiletto boots. She made a remark as she chuckled, "I can't wait to see you in a year after your baby is born and then see what you are wearing."

While my round belly continued to blossom, I also began to enjoy my new fashion phase of "stylish mommy-to-be." The persona of how a mommy-to-be looks, thankfully, has evolved. No longer do you have to settle for a tent-like article of clothing to make you appear and feel bigger than you really are, but now, with the art of ruching (gathered) fabric closely forming around and accenting your beautiful belly (which you would normally endeavor to hide), you have the benefit of no longer having to worry about sucking in your stomach! It was wonderful to experience this new sense of freedom.

However, I started to realize that my black leather stiletto boots would have to take a back seat to the black patent flat shoes I picked up a month before I was pregnant despite the fact they were a size too big (I couldn't resist the amazing sale). Wow, who would have thought they would be essential for the months ahead?

There are so many first moments of my pregnancy carved and etched within my memory that I am sure will make me smile, cry or even laugh in the years to come. On December 23, as we drove to visit family for Christmas, I felt my little one moving within me for the first time. I liked to imagine her as a ballerina, dancing on her tip-toes with such grace and poise. Soon the flutters began to increase with greater intensity and turn into little kicks and stretches that were visible on my round belly of a stage. She sure captivated the audience of her mommy and daddy as we would watch her display her talent, moving and grooving night after night.

On January 5th, we experienced our second ultrasound, a.k.a. "A Peak in the Pod." Unlike the last debut, this one showed her peaceful disposition as she cuddled with her head resting on my placenta as her pillow. We were hoping to find out the gender of our baby, but she was quite content in dreamland. Then, all of a sudden she began to stretch and awake from her sleep and we caught a glimpse of whether we were having a boy or girl. The technician said, "I think you can go out and buy pink."

My husband and I had tears in our eyes and the "daddy to be" questioned, "Are you sure it can't grow anything?" In our hearts we had thought it was a girl, and now we knew for sure that a little princess was on her way.

A Little Thing Called Hope

IT FELT AS IF I had been pregnant forever. As my due date was getting closer and closer the months did go by fast, though, with all the preparations being made, going to the childbirth classes and experiencing the pure joy of getting the baby's room ready. The first treasure I purchased for my little one was from a unique gift place in Florida. There it was, in a purple box with silver writing that read "expressions from the heart." When I opened it up, I found an exquisite heart ornament with Swarovski crystals covering the decorative piece that was embedded in a case lined with attractively gathered gorgeous green fabric. The glistening treasure was a reflection of the delight in my heart for the little miracle of life that was growing and forming inside my womb—both so beautiful, lovely and fragile.

I am so glad that I opened up my heart to allow another human's heart to be discovered, one made from two hearts coming together and God breathing His breath of life as it began to beat. No dream job or career, no Gucci shoe, no amazing musical, nothing material could ever compare to the connection, love and emotion I felt towards this tiny person who had already captured my whole heart.

The waiting period was almost over. I looked as if I was about to burst, but that didn't stop me from running around shopping and picking up little things here and there and spending time with friends at a ladies' tea. The setting was so pretty and quaint as all the décor and table trimmings were aligned so beautifully for the occasion. They had a little contest for the best story and I took home first prize. Another friend of mine, who was due a few weeks later than me, was also there, and someone decided they had better take this opportunity to take a picture of the first time mothers-to-be. I still recall how we posed for a side view of our bellies. It was such a blessing to have a close friend with whom to go through all the first moments that a mother-to-be experiences. So many times we would spill out our hearts to each other with such a newly found understanding and connection that grew as our babies were being fashioned inside our wombs.

That was how the fun began that day and continued throughout the evening. My husband thought it would be a great idea to go on a little date before the baby arrived, as I was due in a week. "How does steak and lobster sound?" he asked, to which my response was one of sheer delight. We went to a wonderful restaurant and enjoyed ourselves immensely. (And yes, I used the excuse that I was eating for two!) After all the excitement from the day, we quietly set off and went to bed, knowing we should take advantage of a little rest and down time, which we knew we would lack in the coming days.

I was peaceful and content in dreamland when, without warning, I woke up to something I had never experienced before. Did I just wet the bed? I looked at the clock and it was 2:30 AM. I quickly woke my husband.

"I think my water just broke," I said to him in disbelief.

His only response was "Are you sure?"

It seemed like the only logical thing that could have happened. I had heard so many other stories of how it occurs, but I never would have thought it would take place in my sleep. For about an hour we gathered everything together for our trip to the hospital. I still remember the calm starlit night. I longed to take it all in and breathe the fresh warm air.

I wanted to savor this moment. "Drive slowly, and can you open the sunroof?" It only took seven minutes to drive to the hospital and I saw no urgency to get there any sooner. We arrived at the hospital safely and in no time at all they checked me out to see how far along I was progressing. The nurses periodically came in to examine me and asked if there was anything I needed to make me more comfortable in the early stages of labor. The contractions were manageable and all was going very smoothly.

After a few hours they moved me into the birthing room. The contractions started to get more intense as the new nurse began her shift for the day and I said good-bye to the one who had gotten me that far. She was the most beautiful blonde nurse, and I thought about how I must have looked right at that moment in my fashionable light blue hospital gown. I guess my discomfort was apparent, because she asked me if I would like an epidural. I declined. Unlike my usual pain tolerance, somehow I was making it through, which even my husband couldn't believe. Eventually, though, I did say yes to a little laughing gas.

Throughout this time the doctor came in here and there. My husband and I were both happy that he wasn't in very often, because his cologne was overpowering and I wasn't comfortable with him. For some reason I had it in my mind that I would deliver this baby without him.

Circumstances led to just that. They realized that there was a possibility that the baby had the umbilical cord wrapped around her neck, so they ordered a pediatrician and an obstetrician to ensure they took all steps necessary to prepare for this delivery. When the obstetrician came in to examine me, I thought I recognized her from somewhere and we remembered meeting each other at my place of employment. She made me feel so at ease and I felt so secure knowing that she would now be the one delivering my baby.

At last the final stages of labor arrived and now it was time to push. I recall saying "I think I need a little help," and minutes later they agreed that the vacuum needed to be utilized. They said if that didn't work then they would have to proceed with a C-section. My husband looked at me with determination and encouraged me, "This is it, honey, you can do it."

Finally, the moment arrived, and our little Hope was born into this world. I will never forget how, as in a twinkling of an eye, it all happened so fast. The doctor apologized to my husband that he wouldn't be allowed to cut the umbilical cord, as they wanted to get it done quickly and make certain the baby was OK. It was as if time had stopped and there I was, watching as they checked to see that all was well with my new baby girl.

My husband stood between us, torn as to whether he should stay at my bedside or attend to our daughter. I could sense the intense feelings of concern and love that he was feeling for his girls as we held each other's hands. I assured him that he needed to go be with our daughter and that I was taken care of. It is funny how in a flash you change from being concerned about yourself to putting your child's needs above your own. I believe it is something that a mother continues to do throughout her lifetime.

Words cannot describe the feelings a new mom experiences as her baby is placed in her arms for the first time. Every little breath, every little smile, every little face—every little expression captivates you. A new little life brings incredible joy to everyone it comes in contact with, and we were very proud parents introducing our little angel to the world. Sure there were sleepless nights and a new routine to get accustomed to, but nothing could extinguish the glow that permeated everything we were experiencing.

I recently found the following paragraphs in my journal. My heart was so full of love for my little Hope and I couldn't help but write down how I felt. It's amazing the amount of love you can feel for such a tiny little infant who has graced your life for only such a short time. Despite all that I have gone through since Hope was born, finding the excerpt below only signifies to me that my love for my daughter was always foremost in my mind.

"There is nothing more beautiful
than being a mother"

Derek and I feel so blessed to have this little miracle of life. She surprised us and came early. I guess she must have heard her Mommy and Daddy saying how we couldn't wait to meet her. What a good little girl. She arrived into the world on Sunday, May 29, 2005, at 12:17 PM. Finally we could hold her in our arms.

Hope's 1st Week...wow, where has all the time gone? What to Expect When You're Expecting *has been put on my bookshelf and replaced with,* Baby Week By Week. *As you go through the first week, you have no time to read, but I enjoyed early this morning to reflect and reminisce on the experience Derek and I have already gone through together. We are starting to realize what Mommy and Daddy and Baby Hope need. We are all there for each other and enjoying the beautiful bond and foundation that is being re-shaped and discovered. We are so blessed! We are amazed at the wonderful support and feel loved. We always knew what Hope's name was to be even before she was conceived, and she is already stepping into her own unique destiny.*

Daddy and I have truly enjoyed your first week's birthday, you amaze us. Not only has our love for one another grown, but also each and every moment we cherish with you. You are Daddy's little girl, but not for a minute does Mommy feel left out, because I have gone from being a Princess to a Queen. Again, I am living out my dreams with my Prince Charming. He's holding and comforting you right now. Mommy will never forget and I will always treasure these memories. I love you so much. Time to feed you, talk soon.

Daddy's always saying Mommy never stops talking. It is so neat to see how you are responding—we're a little biased, but you are gorgeous and such a smart baby. We are learning what your cries mean and desire to give you all you need. We enjoy extravagant living, but now I realize it isn't dollars and cents. It is enjoying life to the fullest and doing what you are passionate about. Always know that we will do all we can to give you the best, our precious little jewel.

Expressions from the heart...Happy first week, you truly capture our hearts.

~XOXO Mommy & Daddy

I never would have thought it possible for something to mar the time and love that I shared with my daughter. Nothing could change this. Or that's what

I thought. Two weeks after Hope was born everything started to become a big blur. I can't call to mind when or why, but suddenly my array of emotions began to turn, and it was an abrupt turn.

I went to Calgary to spend time with my thirteen-day-old granddaughter and help out wherever I could. Shortly after I arrived, my daughter-in-law, Gen, asked me if she could go upstairs to have a shower and get dressed up. She said I was used to looking frumpy, but she liked to look nice.

That was my first clue something was wrong. I later looked up "frump" in the dictionary: "a woman who is shabby and out of style in dress." This would be a term Gen would be familiar with, having been employed in the fashion industry. Fashion and clothes have never been important to me and I do dress very simple, but that was not something Gen would normally say to me.

Quite some time later she called down from upstairs and said she couldn't stay up there any longer and asked if she could come downstairs. I said of course, since it was her home. I gave her a hug and she got very emotional and stated she had some concerns about being able to care for her baby. I told her I would help her in any way I could, and she seemed to settle. She appeared to be relieved to have me caring for the baby.

When Derek came home from work, we were having a general conversation when Gen spoke out things that had nothing to do with what we were talking about. When Derek questioned where that had come from, Gen started to cry and couldn't stop. My thoughts were that she was sleep-deprived, and if I took care of the baby and she got rest she would be fine. Derek said she hadn't been sleeping and that when she could have been sleeping he'd found her looking at the baby.

The second day I was there, Gen's family members were also all there and engaged in a conversation in the kitchen that involved a lot of laughter. I was sitting in the living room by myself and noticed that Gen was becoming very agitated. She came to me and told me I had to ask them all to leave. Gen is very close to all her family and loves them dearly, so this surprised me. I said, "This is your home and your family, I can't tell them to leave. If you are tired and want to rest, then ask them to leave."

She told them she wanted them to leave, but no one really noticed her. She was becoming more agitated and came to me again and asked me to tell them. I went and found Derek and explained to him what was happening, so he asked them to leave. At this point she was somewhat withdrawn from the baby and did not appear comfortable with the breastfeeding. Derek helped her pump some milk so I could do the night feeding and Gen could get some rest. She went to bed early and didn't come downstairs until noon the next day.

She never went near the baby, but came right to me and said she needed help. I told her I knew she did, but it was Sunday and we would take her to her doctor the next morning. She said she couldn't wait until tomorrow and that she needed help now. She went to a magnet on the fridge and said, "I can call this number anytime for help," and picked up the phone and called the number for Early Start. They must have asked if she was alone, because she said her husband and his mother were there. They talked to her for a while, then asked to speak to Derek. They told him he had to take her to the Rockyview General Hospital Emergency as soon as possible, for they had a postpartum depression program there. Gen wanted to leave right away, but Derek wanted to quickly have something to eat first. Gen said she needed to go "now!" and left the house without any shoes on and started walking down the street.

After being seen by several doctors in emergency, she was diagnosed with postpartum psychosis and admitted under the Mental Health Act. I called the same helpline Gen called, as I was not sure how much and how often the feedings should be. I was told the person Gen reached when she called the helpline had a lot of experience in postpartum depression, so that was fortunate. When Derek finally arrived home from the hospital at midnight, my heart ached for him when he told me the last thing he ever expected in his life to see was his wife being admitted to a Psych unit. How difficult it was for him to leave her that night!

The doctors wanted the baby to be at the hospital the next day to try and help Gen keep in touch with reality. Genevieve would not cooperate with taking the medication, so they had to restrain her and give it by injection, which was extremely upsetting for her (and upsetting for us to experience too, even though we were outside the room). The next day, Derek got a phone call saying she wasn't responding to the medication. They wanted him there with the baby to see if that would help, and if not, they were going to have to use ECT. Derek called Gen's parents to keep them *informed, and they were extremely against ECT and forbid Derek to consent to it. The doctor explained to us that it was a life-threatening medical emergency, as the brain can only stay in that state so long before it will shut down.*

I will never forget the turmoil Derek went through that day. Thankfully, Gen's sister, who is a nurse, her brothers and the Pastor from their church agreed that God would help to heal her but required some medical intervention, and they all supported the treatment. The doctor told Derek that Genevieve had been admitted under the Mental Health Act, and the treatment would be done with or without his consent. The explanation they gave us about ECT was that it is like rebooting a computer to unscramble the brain.

We took the baby to the hospital every day for Gen to spend time with her. Many days in Gen's mind it wasn't her baby and Derek wasn't her husband. I'm not sure who she thought I was. It was so sad when we would leave the hospital unit and see her in the hall watching us leave. Most days Derek went to the hospital twice a day, which was a thirty-minute drive each way. I can only imagine how difficult and exhausting those two months were for him, being at the hospital with Gen as much as he could, spending time with his new daughter and trying to keep up with his work. He had unbelievable support from his employer and was given whatever time he needed. My sister was also a huge support and made many trips to the hospital with the baby and I so Derek could spend more time at work.

Derek never attempted to keep any of Gen's illness from anyone, and as a result had unending support and prayers from family, friends, church and employers. I am thankful I was able to be there for Derek and Gen to provide care for Hope and look after their home, as I sensed Gen trusted me. Life takes some crazy directions—sometimes causing changes in our lives that we can't anticipate—but even though we try to cope as best we can, some things are beyond our control.

It was sad to see what the drugs had done to Gen's appearance. She showed a lot of courage and strength and worked very hard to get well. She also received excellent care from Dr. Petrov. Whenever Dr. Petrov was around while we were at the hospital, she took time to talk with us and inquire about our well-being and whether or not there was anything we needed. She had endless praise for Derek's support and devotion to Gen.

It was a horrendous time for Gen, Derek and their families, but thankfully Gen was able to be free of the medications, recover from her illness and be a loving and devoted mother to her precious daughter. Hope was so appropriately named, as in the beginning the prognosis was not great, but we always had HOPE.

~Brenda

I first met Genevieve when she and her family were in the midst of a crisis. Genevieve and her husband had just welcomed their baby girl into the world after an uncomplicated pregnancy and delivery, but in the midst of a celebration things went terribly wrong. Genevieve was brought to the hospital.

What struck me at the time was the united feeling of fear in the patient and her husband:

fear of facing what was happening to them and the difficulty in understanding it and coping with it. There was also fear of the future, fear for the baby, and fear for their lives together. It was with the same fear that they helplessly watched how Genevieve struggled to do what she had easily done even a few days before, like holding the baby and feeding her with a bottle. It was with the same fear that they listened to the explanation of the diagnosis, treatment suggestions and its potential risks for Genevieve.

However, from the first moments there was another feeling, even stronger than the fear, and that was their trust and support of each other. I believe it was that support and trust that helped Genevieve and her family to get through this terrible ordeal.

~Dr. Petrov

A Shattered Dream

I REMEMBER ONE NIGHT talking to my mom on the phone, hidden in my closet, crying uncontrollably. I can still feel the concern in my mother's voice as she caught a glimpse of the state I was in, asked me where Hope was and encouraged me to ensure she was being taken care of. A mother always knows when something doesn't seem right. It was from that point on that I took a downward spiral.

Before Hope was born I couldn't wait to have my baby shower, but when it came to the actual morning of the shower, I didn't even want to get out of bed. I think back to how I felt as my mom and sister-in-law came into my room to try and help me get ready. It was so out of my character to not want to be around people. That day it seemed like someone had put me in a bubble. Everyone was all around me, but I was not really there, or so it seemed. From that moment on my memory is scattered, with bits and pieces missing and locked away from what I can recall.

I can still picture the hospital room and its nice big windows that overlooked the river. Unit 49—my home for a couple of months. (Never would I have dreamed that I would spend my summer there.) Before Hope was born I envisioned myself enjoying walks with her, strolling around the water pond behind our home. Instead, I had to ask to attain a pass to even take a walk on the path behind the hospital. It was like being locked up in a cell, and ironically, that is how I felt, like a bird in a cage trapped in my own body—a cage with no escape.

I recall one evening listening to my iPod in my hospital room. I thought I was in a recording studio and that the window was the sound booth. I sang my heart out and intended to make a great recording. I laugh now at the silliness of it all, but the harsh reality was I was going out of my mind.

My husband was so supportive. The nurses said it was easier for me to take my medication at night if he was there, as he brought me peace and comfort. It was very difficult for him, and he got frustrated one night as he watched his wife go through the horrible ordeal. "It is like I am living in a Hollywood horror movie," he remarked, but the truth was apparent when he was asked to leave the room since I was being difficult and not cooperating and taking my medication. The medication wasn't totally effective, so the doctors needed to take further measures.

The next form of treatment they administered to me, Electroconvulsive Therapy (ECT), continues to be surrounded by a lot of controversy, and my family was torn as to whether this should be allowed. When I think of this treatment, what plays in my head is a picture of Frankenstein getting zapped!

It was a beautiful day in June of 2005, and while I was in my studio, the phone rang.

"Mom, what year is it?"

"I was married to Derek, but now I'm not."

"Am I Gen, Genevieve, or Geni?"

"You always told me the truth, who am I?"

The medical professionals determined that our daughter Genevieve was diagnosed with an extreme case of postpartum psychosis and made the decision for her to begin a series of reoccurring ECT treatments. Unfamiliar with the procedures and statistics, as Genevieve's parents it was like a death sentence to us, for we could only relate to "One Flew Over the Cuckoo's Nest." One could only imagine our emotions—she was our little princess.

Upon arrival in Calgary, we proceeded to Rockyview General Hospital Unit 49 Psychiatric Ward, where our family gathered around Genevieve as she sat up in her bed. The specialist entered and Genevieve excitedly gave her introductions. "This is my brother, Chris, and his girlfriend, my brother, Tom, and his wife Kari, and my sweet sister, Elisa. Oh no, where's Dustin?!"

"It's OK, he's working. He will come," Elisa calmed her.

"This is my Mom, oh where's Dad! Is he dead?"

"No, Gen, Dad is on his way and will be with you shortly," I replied.

After my husband's arrival, we proceeded into the conference room to gain some insight through a video on ECT. Elisa stayed back in the room with her sister, singing songs of encouragement. Many patients walked by the closed door of Gen's room to hear what they thought was an angel. As a family, we later brought the evening to a close by singing:

> *...Come in empty*
> *I leave filled*
> *Bring my sickness*
> *And I leave healed*
> *Broken hearted*
> *You mend every piece*
> *Come in captive*
> *and I leave free...*[2]

Due to the extreme pressures of Derek's consistent hospital visits and the emotions he faced with a wife who didn't know him as her husband, Genevieve's Dad, Wes, and I decided to relieve him, and a plan was put into place. Other precious family members would rotate and tend to baby Hope, and we would focus on surrounding Geni in the hospital three to four days a week, or, as she would say, "Gen, Genevieve, or am I Geni?"

No one fully understood the extremity of her condition as we would listen to Genevieve talk. Her intelligent mind was still evident as she verbalized her thoughts, only now she spoke at an unusually high rate of speed. The complexity of the brain is amazing. What more did we know to do? Understanding that words are powerful, we would speak, "Shalom, Shalom," over and over again, believing just what it means: "nothing missing, nothing broken."

---

[2] Woodley, Laura. "This is Life" © 2002 Laura Woodley. All rights reserved. International copyright secured. CCLI song #4385761. Used by permission.

Though we spoke it under our breath, she would on occasion ask, "How come Dad always says, 'Shalom, Shalom?'" There was a peace breaking through for us as well, even though the physical evidence was still dim.

The ECT treatments were unknown to Genevieve, and she would wonder why there was gel on her temples and in her hair and tape around her wrists. The voltage would erase her memory of all she knew at that time. Even so, she maintained her sense of perfection by making sure all the greeting cards in the ward were lined up from smallest to tallest.

Visitation was allowed for immediate family only, since too many faces would only confuse her more. How fear can grip a mind! Upon entering her room, many times we would find her suitcases and the hospital chairs placed in front of the electrical outlets to protect her baby. Unlike most cases, Genevieve was overprotective of everyone's wellbeing. She was rare in the fact that she never wanted to take her own life. Colors meant a lot to Gen—pink and purple were her favorite. Orange was not a good color, because it reminded her of a school bus and she thought she had to go back to school since all her writing and reading skills had faded to a minimum.

The day came when we brought her some special shampoo and she finally felt that it would be alright to have a shower on her own with the curtain down in place. Progression was showing, and I chanced bringing her a new tube of lipstick she had purchased before having the baby. These were daily things that we normally wouldn't think twice about, but standing and watching Geni willingly turn in her tube of lipstick to the front desk at the end of the day, I realized that all freedom was restrained. It would bring us some laughter later, when we noticed that Unit 49 seemed to be looking a little brighter, as many started dressing up and putting on their own lipstick. A few began to ask when Gen's family was coming back to visit her. Often, a fellow patient, singing "Sweet Genevieve," would hover around us.

As Genevieve's mom, I was a hit with the patients, but I was not one of the doctor's favorites. Gen was not partial to open therapy sessions and would convince me to get her a pass. Off to shopping we would go, exactly where I was not to take her. Upon return, they required an explanation as to why we were late. Though I'd taken care to take her to a quieter venue, it was never believed that I was delayed by traffic.

"So, Genevieve," I would ask, "which outfit did you like?"

Again she would say, "I can't remember."

Back in her hospital room in Unit 49, we would color Cinderella felt art together, as this was the level that her mind was at. "Cinderella" was the same theme to which Genevieve and Derek had walked down the aisle seven years prior on their wedding day.

As word got out it was often asked, "How are you doing?" "Is Derek going to leave her?"

Our replies would stay the same.

"Yes, we are all fine."

"All will be well and Derek remains her Prince."

"In faith, yes, she will be totally healed in time."

"Nothing missing, nothing broken."

Often we would be leaving her room as she laid her head down for the night. With tears streaming down her cheeks onto her pillow, she would try to sing slowly, line by line, "God is too wise to be mistaken, God is too good to be unkind. If the pathway grows dim and you just can't see Him, trust His heart."[3] It was her own therapy, as she would sing worship songs with her iPod.

The time came for the Taylor's to take their family holiday in the USA. Under doctor's orders, Genevieve could not leave the country; in fact, she was not permitted to leave the city of Calgary. To compensate, our family took her to Heritage Park. We wanted to sneak her back to Medicine Hat on a weekend pass, but as transparent as Genevieve was, she would have been the first to tell the doctor on us. No secrets were ever withheld by Geni.

Upon exiting the secured hospital unit doors as usual, I would often say, "Call me, honey, if you want to talk," so soon to forget that the response would be, "I don't know how." The everyday tasks of remembering phone numbers and not mixing up names were part of the game. "Oh, there's so and so walking down the hall in the ward," she'd say as she would confuse a fellow patient with someone she knew from her past. A friendly, "Hello" was her gift to everyone she greeted, and she looked like a gem shining more radiant than ever as her condition was improving.

---

[3] Mason, Babbie and Carswell, Eddie. "Trust His Heart" © 1989 Dayspring Music, LLC (a div. of Word Music Group, Inc.) / May Sun Music (Admin. by Word Music Group, Inc.) / Word Music, LLC (a div. of Word Music Group, Inc.) / Causing Change Music (Admin. by Word Music Group, Inc.). All rights reserved. Used by permission.

As *Genevieve's parents, we would like to extend a special thank-you to all of the friends, family and colleagues who supported Genevieve and continue to believe in her and to the medical professionals (especially Dr. Petrov) for their care. Most of all, our thanks to Genevieve, who taught us to love and treasure the gift of life, and to our granddaughter Hope, who brings hope to the hopeless. They are God's Gifts to us.*

~Wes & Peggy Aman

THROUGH IT ALL
Healing Praise

MY HUSBAND WAS TOLD by the doctors that he was left with no choice in regards to my treatment.

"Your wife isn't responding to the medication and we deem her a medical emergency. If you do not consent to this, this will go to the courts." I can't imagine having to make all those decisions, but then, in the midst of it all there really was no choice.

I had an ECT treatment every Monday, Wednesday and Friday on a weekly basis, but I can only call to mind the last treatment. The nurse woke me early that morning and asked me to get into the blue hospital gown. I remember walking with the nurse down the cold hall into the treatment room. There in that room, I lay down on the bed and they hooked me up to all the monitors and covered me with a warm blanket. The anesthesiologist wore a green cap and I can still picture all the medical staff that provided assistance in the procedure, but it felt like a weird dream.

I counted to ten and I was put to sleep. I woke in my room hours later as I recovered from the treatment. To this day, I still can't believe that I was put through that process on my path to recovery. You know those times when you wish you could take back what you just said, or you would like to go back in time and do it differently? In this instance, it was beyond my control and I couldn't have prevented it from occurring. The only thing I can do now is to move on, live with the realization that the doctors and medical staff saw it necessary and be thankful that I am not living with any side affects except for memory loss. I realize now what my limits are without putting limits on what I can accomplish in my goals and aspirations. What you have been through can change you, and it is your choice and attitude that will either make you shine or allow your heartache to consume you and take your life away.

so ce

Worship continued to bring me strength, and my heart would be touched as tears would stream down my face as I would listen to the songs. My husband would ask me, "Did you enjoy the Michael W. Smith concert?" and to this day I cannot bring to mind even being there. With my memory locked away, I had no recollection of being at a worship concert, yet the healing it brought me is undeniable as the "Healing Rain"[4] flowed. Some people say it is maybe a blessing to not recall that painful time in my life and that it is simply life's way of protecting me.

---

[4] At that concert Michael W. Smith performed the song "Healing Rain" written by Martin Smith, Matthew Ryan Bronleewe and Michael W. Smith ©2004 Curious? Music UK (Admin. by EMI Christian Music Publishing) Word Music, LLC (a div. of Word Music Group, Inc.) Smittyfly Music (Admin. by Word Music Group, Inc.) Songs From The Farm Windswept Pacific Music Ltd.

I awakened from my treatments with only segments of my stay in Unit 49 firmly etched in my mind. The beginning and the end will forever be in my memory, but everything in-between is like it never really took place. During the last week before I was discharged, I remember looking at the people around me who were patients at that time and feeling such compassion for them. They just seemed so lost, so distant. I wished I could help them so they, too, could be free from their pain. My heart's aspiration is to be an encouragement to those around me, as those close to me have been there for me.

I had already been in the hospital psych ward (being treated for post-partum psychosis) for approximately 6 weeks. I was feeling terrified, lost in my own tormented delusions and very frightened about my future.

Then one evening, while walking down the hospital corridor hallways (which was one of my usual ways to pass the time), I heard the most beautiful, angelic voice coming from the room down the hall from me. It was like I heard an angel singing the most beautiful worship songs. I couldn't believe it!

It was a time when I felt my darkest despair and I felt as if God had left me, but there in the hospital was someone singing worship songs. (Trust me, you do not usually hear beautiful worship songs in the psych ward—you usually hear people talking nonsense and crazy chatter to themselves as they pace the hallways frantically.) I remember at the time thinking if I could only go into the room where the singing was coming from I could forget my troubles, and even for a fleeting moment my spirit would be lifted. Later on, I learned that it was Genevieve who had been singing and that she was being treated for postpartum psychosis, just like me.

"Wow!" I thought, "That girl is so amazing. She is being treated for psychosis, like me, but she can still sing like that." I had been so unwell and couldn't have carried on a conversation with someone, never mind singing!

Often I walked past Genevieve's room, wanting to talk to her and let her know how amazing her singing was. But every time I walked past her room, she was asleep or still recovering from the shock treatments she was getting. On my second last day in the hospital, we sat together for a brief moment, but I was still unable to talk to Genevieve, because she was still caught in the awful disease of psychosis (same as I had been in) which robs your very self from you.

Later on, before I checked out of the hospital, my mom was able to get Genevieve's phone number from her mother. I remember at the time being so embarrassed that my mom was being so forward as to ask for a stranger's phone number, but what a blessing it has been to get to know Genevieve.

I finally got enough courage to call her, because I am kind of shy at first, especially calling strangers...eh hem...what do you say? "You don't know me, but I was in the hospital with you and I was wondering if you want to get together for a visit?"

God has given me a wonderful friend, Genevieve, who I can share, cry and laugh with about things that others may not understand. Genevieve is one of the most beautiful, wonderful people, with an amazing voice to top it off. I feel very privileged to have her as one of my friends.

~Caryn

THROUGH IT ALL

Amazing Grace

EVEN THOUGH I HAVE LOST many memories, one dear friend's effort to do something special for me still stands apart. The picture has never left my recollection—she created an indoor picnic for Hope and I in my living room! The freshly cut fruit, her delicious cuisine and the tender love and care she put into the details were exceptional. It reminds me that every now and then we need to step out and do something unique, even though we may never fully see the impact and lasting impression it may have. Sometimes it means being transparent when we would like to put on a façade or just pretend like everything is perfect.

Before this, it was difficult for me to be real. I would rather be perceived as perfect. I always had to coordinate the perfect outfit, perform a perfect song and be a perfect weight. It is not wrong to want to obtain and do things in excellence, but when the power to perform takes all the beauty away, then it becomes a problem.

Through my illness I was stripped of my conception of perfection. When I would look in the mirror I would be conscious of my weight as I gained more than when I was pregnant. Due to a side effect of my medication, my skin would break out, and the result has been a few scars, which even the best make-up is unable to conceal. Sure, I still have the desire to put together a beautiful outfit, but I couldn't get over how I looked. Somehow, during my stay at the hospital, my body was switched with someone I never imagined I would have to meet in the mirror every day.

They say true beauty lies within, and I understand the truth in that statement now that I have been healed from deep inside my innermost being. Now the transformation is shown as the new me radiates—it is like I died and was reborn.

When it was time to be released from the hospital and go home, I remember talking with my mother–in–law and my husband about having a personal care assistant to help me during the day while my husband was at work. At first I was a little resistant, as I did not think this was necessary, but now, when I look back, I am so thankful for the wonderful assistance I received that month.

The personal care assistant who came was just what I needed, and I did not feel awkward, but felt at ease as she showed me how to get Hope on a schedule and to make things go smoothly. I was still very heavily medicated at the time and took long naps while Hope was resting. She helped me get into the new routine of balancing baby, daily routines and ensuring I was being taken care of. This served as a reminder that my pride had been extinguished. How did I know this? Before I went into the hospital I would insist on doing everything on my own, not wanting to take help from anyone offering to lend a hand. Now I was more than willing to take any kind of help that was offered, and I found myself having no issues with this.

As my doctor began weaning me off my medication, I started to work out with a personal trainer, and it was with persistence and healthy eating that I started to return to the figure I once had. I understand what it is like to go through the all-consuming battle of the weight issue. As I continued, I began feeling more and more like myself again, but I knew I had changed. I had developed into someone who takes life's song and begins to write the incredible display of grace as a new page unfolds.

Grace, yes "Amazing Grace." The song has been heard throughout many generations, but one day it felt fresh, like spring rain bouncing as it pitter-patters on anything it touches. It was refreshing spirit-to-spirit worship where I connected and sensed God's awesome presence surrounding me as I inhaled and took it all in. It wasn't just the creative version and arrangement of the old hymn that provoked this newness, but it was a moment where I could hear the heartbeat of God as He whispered His promises to me—what I call a "now moment" of worship.

After that more inspired ideas began to awaken, and ironically, it all took place where dream bubbles rupture and take flight into reality—at the Dream Centre in my hometown of Medicine Hat. I guess you sometimes need to revisit where you came from and recall the aspirations concealed inside your heart before you can really move forward with the dream that God has birthed within you.

A two-fold dream started to unravel at that point in time, and from then on I moved forward to grasp and take hold of my future endeavors while continuing to place my life and my dreams into God's sovereign hands.

My family has known Gen's family since before either of us were born. Gen and I became good friends once we hit high school. We hung out at youth group and were involved in various church musicals. Even as graduation from high school came and went, we remained good friends. We saw each other through many good times and many hardships. We enjoyed our courtships and were bridesmaids for each other.

Wow, how time flies! It is now nine years of marriage and four children (plus one on the way) later. There were times since marriage and babies entered the picture where Gen and I wouldn't connect for a couple of months, but the beauty of true friendship is that it didn't matter. We would pick up right where we left off.

When Gen and Derek told us they were pregnant, Dave and I were so excited for them. I honestly did not know if Gen was ever going to want children. To be honest, I was also wondering how she was going to be as a mom. She is not the stereotypical soccer mom. Gen and Derek's house was definitely not kid-friendly. They had white carpet and glass tables!

I remember when our second son was six weeks old. Dave and I were up for a conference, and our son, who was born premature, had to go for a test at the children's hospital. Gen took our older son, who at that time would have been just under a year, shopping during the test, and I remember Gen talking about how she couldn't figure out how to make the stroller work. She always seemed uncomfortable when she was holding our kids, like she wasn't sure what to do with them.

We received a call from Derek when Hope was born and were thrilled they had a girl. It was not until a couple of weeks later that we heard from some other mutual friends that Gen had become very ill and was hospitalized. I phoned Derek right away, and we just hurt with him for all they were going through. I am a nurse and had suffered through postpartum depression with my second child, but it was nothing in comparison to the turmoil their family was in.

I immediately felt like we should go see Gen, so that weekend we drove up to Calgary. Thankfully, at that time Gen was able to take some day passes, so we were able to visit with her and Hope in her own home.

Gen was very quiet, and her speech and all of her actions seemed as if they were in slow motion. She seemed very detached. If you knew Gen before, you knew she was definitely a go-getter and liked to talk. It's hard to watch someone you know and love walk through such an awful thing, and yet, I have seen God move powerfully in Gen's life.

Once Gen had Hope and was feeling well again, I remember visiting her with our baby girl.

Such contrast! Gen was making dinner (the fridge used to be bare bones) and there were toys all over the floor. I commented on how funny it was to see her being so domestic. Their home has been transformed into a toy store in which my kids love to play and feel right at home.

She is such an attentive, loving mother. She is generous with her time and resources. Jesus Christ is at the center of her life and she walks out her faith in such a way that God uses her to encourage me every time we have the chance to visit. I believe God does not give us anything we cannot handle, and watching Gen come out of this health crisis free and clear of medication, with a restored mind and stronger than ever in her faith is true testament to the love and grace of God. Gen is now seeing the desires of her heart come to pass. I thank the Lord I can call her my friend.

~Jen

At the time when I was very sick, my husband and I were ready to put our dreams to rest about ever having another child. We never again wanted to relive the pain that we were going through, but as we continued to walk together on our path of parenthood all the fear began to diminish and our thoughts became clear. We truly enjoyed being parents and our desire to have a brother or sister for Hope was beginning to burn within our hearts all over again, just as the yearning and longing had risen the first time.

As the new year of 2007 began, we decided to give it a try. Over the past year we had already been discussing and planning with my doctors for this next pregnancy. Later, in March, we were so excited to find out that we were having another baby. Telling people the news was a little different this time, as we knew some would think we were crazy to take the chance of postpartum psychosis happening again, since there is a 60-70 percent rate of re-occurrence. Somehow we had a peace that no matter what would come our way, we would hold onto hope and the peace that passes all understanding.

Just like every child is unique and different in his or her own special way, so it is true that my second pregnancy has had its own distinctive characteristics. Knowing that there is a little life blooming inside with its own distinguishing personality and a purpose and destiny that cannot be duplicated—a rare matchless gem—is remarkable.

Before Hope was even conceived, I knew what her name was to be, and in the same way I was determined to find the perfect name for this new little miracle. We chose Paige Grace for a girl, but somehow we found it more difficult to agree on a boy's name. One evening I deliberated and out of nowhere mentioned the name Zachary Ty to my husband. Finally we were both in agreement, and so I went to my laptop and did a name search to find out the meaning of this name. Zachary Ty came up meaning "Remembered by God," and I just sat there with tears forming in the corners of my eyes. I was powerfully reminded that even before we were born,

God breathed His purpose and destiny in us, and that
He has an exclusive plan for each one of our lives.

"CALLED"

Wake up in the morning
Sunlight on my face
You're found ever faithful
God You never change
The gift of every heartbeat
You're not done with me yet
Each day's an invitation
Christ in every breath

Called by You, Called to live
Called by love, Called to give
All my life to You, Lord
Called by name, To follow You
Called to love

You welcome little children
Hold them in Your arms
You speak words of blessing
Such life reveals God's heart
You speak into existence
Before it is to be
Signed, sealed with purpose
From the King, You, to me

Trusting and resting
The journey is long
Gone before, now You're leading me on
Author, perfector
Shape now my faith
Jesus Your unfailing way

© 2007 DAVID MORIN & GENEVIEVE TAYLOR

The song "I Am Not Forgotten"[5] began to play in my heart during that moment, and I will never forget how clear and distinctive it was—like a ground-breaking revelation of something I had known my whole life, but suddenly the light bulb went on. I started to really comprehend the meaning of what God was trying to convey. No matter how you were conceived, God knew you and with all His creativity thought of you. Though we may bear similar personalities, we are each "one of a kind."

As I was growing up with my two brothers and one sister, I remarked how my parents treated each one of us as unique. They instilled in us that we need to follow the passions that burn inside of us, fulfill our heart's desires and use our own distinct gifts. That's why I guess I want to find the perfect name for each one of my children. Just like my parents did for me and my siblings, I know that I will allow and encourage each of my children to be their own person, pursuing and fulfilling their own unique dreams.

Nothing could have prepared me for the experience I would encounter when I walked into the room to see my sister for the first time at the hospital in the psychiatric unit. The person who, growing up, I had always looked up to and, in certain ways, tried to be more like, was not the

---

[5] Houghton, Israel and Lindsay, Aaron. "I Am Not Forgotten" © 2005 Integrity's Praise! Music, Sound Of The New Breed, Aaron Lindsey Publishing.

person I saw there on that day. Someone who always knew who she was and what she wanted, now, in that bed, was someone who thought she was someone else. Whenever we talked about her new child or her life, she would look at me and respond "No, that's your baby, that's your life. I don't have a baby, you do." No matter how hard we tried, there was no convincing her of the truth.

It was hard to see how all the childhood memories, both good and bad, were now being scrambled in her mind's eye as though they were all happening to her again. It was like chaos and confusion in her mind—nothing made sense. Was this a joke? Was this really happening to my sister? Would she ever be herself again? So many questions came to mind—questions that not even the doctors could answer. Yet, in the midst of this confusion, it was comforting to know that through worship the peace of God could still be felt...the "peace that passes all understanding." In that hospital room that day, I began to sing worship songs to God, and it did not take long for Gen to join in. The peace and presence of God that we had so often felt in times before was now embracing us that day. No matter where this took us, we were going to make it.

Although the months that followed were not easy, we drew strength from God's Word. No matter what kind of a report we received, I kept speaking the promises of God over Gen. "God has not given her a spirit of fear, but of love, power, and a sound mind."

Whenever I had days off from work, I had the opportunity to take care of Hope. Never before having any children of my own, looking after a newborn was a new adventure in itself! The task was made even more challenging by, on a daily basis, getting Hope ready, with a diaper bag full of essentials, to take her to visit her mom. Some of those visits consisted of Gen staring deep into space as she held her precious little baby in her arms. We believed, however, that it was important for both of them to spend time together to help encourage their bonding. Over time, it was apparent that Gen was improving by the way she started to show more interest in and be more comfortable with Hope.

When Gen was discharged from the hospital, she was still not well enough to take care of Hope by herself. Someone always had to be with her. Whenever Derek went out of town for business, someone would either stay with them in Calgary or, on a number of occasions, Gen and Hope would come to Medicine Hat and stay with me. During those visits, I noticed that, even when Gen was doing "good," deep in my heart I knew she was not completely "herself" again. This person, who before was always outgoing, talkative, full of life and energy and who always looked and dressed her best, was now like a zombie—lifeless and expressionless. It was a chore for me to struggle to carry on a conversation with her.

I remember the feelings of joy and excitement that rose within me the moment I realized my sister was back to herself. The life within her overflowed from the inside out, sparkled in her eyes, enlightened her expressions and became apparent in her speech. Praise God, my sister was back! And it was not only that she was herself, she was better. Through this experience, her character grew as God molded her into a person full of mercy, grace and compassion.

Whatever circumstances you may be facing today, God wants you to know you can trust Him. Whatever desire you hold in your heart, know that he can perform miracles in your life.

~Elisa

The Forming of a Dream

As I reminisce about my childhood, I recall many times when my siblings and I would set up for our very own church service in our living room with the rock marble fireplace for our backdrop. I would get out my turquoise blue worship book, lay it out on the office chair and usher in the presence of God through my heartfelt worship. My little brother would play the keyboard and my sister would end with a powerful preaching of the Word (using her little white Bible even before she could read). All this was being captured as my other brother would do the audio and record it all on our tape deck.

As parents, we need to allow and support our children and see what sparks in their imagination so we can pray that God will utilize these tiny embers that burn from deep within. The power of a spoken word needs to bring life, and too often we see the opposite occur.

Life, this voyage on earth, can be here today and gone tomorrow. I know without a shadow of a doubt that God takes care of our every need. The song "So In Need" is playing on my iTunes right now, and once again I am vividly reminded how much I can rely on my Heavenly Father to take care of all my needs.

"SO IN NEED"[6]
by Sherilyn Keller

With a broken heart, I come to stand before You
I'm so in need of a comforting love
I'm feeling lost and I'm tired of feeling empty
I'm so in need of you, I'm so in need of You

Now I'm holding on to the one that gives me hope
Jesus, how I need You
Oh, this stirring in my soul, just won't let me go
Because I know, I'm so in need of You

It's hard to trust and fear whelms up within me
I'm so in need of a comforting love
I need Your love and Your presence all around me
I'm so in need of You, I'm so in need of You

No matter how I try, I could never live without You
Forgive me for thinking I can make it on my own

This morning I was taken back to the time I was asked to sing at a little girl's funeral. As I sang "If You Could See Me Now,"[7] there her mom sat, a foot away from me, so broken. But somehow, as I sang the words, she was comforted by knowing that her daughter was now being cared for by Something or

[6] Keller, Sherrilyn. "So In Need" © 2003 Mercy / Vineyard Publishing (Admin. by Music Services). All rights reserved. Used by permission.

[7] Noblitt, Kim. "If You Could See Me Now" © 1992 Hold Onto Music (Admin. by Integrity's! Praise Music)/Integrity's Praise! Music.

Someone higher, even though she couldn't fully comprehend it, since she'd never had a personal relationship with the Giver of Life. I felt to write down the words to the song (which I changed slightly from the original version to make it more suitable for a young child) on a beautiful piece of stationary for her, so she could go back and be reminded and somehow cling to hope that her daughter was in a heavenly place.

There is something powerful when you can remember but at the same time move on. Once more, I praise with nothing left within me but His strength and promise that He will yet again see me through. Psalm 71:14 expresses my heart, "But as for me, I will always have hope; I will praise you more and more."

"MORE AND MORE"

Circumstances don't determine
Whether I will praise

I will praise You more and more
I will praise like never before
Pow'r and glory on display
Praise prepares the way

I will praise You more and more
I will praise like never before
Memory that never fades
Your name and Your renown

I will praise You

© 2007 GENEVIEVE TAYLOR & MIRANDA BROWN

Even though I would like to be bitter and ask God "Why did this have to happen?" I instead choose to put on a garment of praise and know that He will continue to guide my steps. I never thought I would have to go through any more difficulties with pregnancies. "Didn't I already go through enough?"

Another chapter in the pages of my life has now been written; I have a new revelation of how life ends if there is no heartbeat. It is a truth that became apparent as the realization of it all became definite while we watched the ultrasound screen.

Right away we knew something wasn't right. There was no dancing, no flicker of life—only a black and white screen. Black and white, and as clear as it could be, it was confirmed as the technician quickly located the doctor. He scanned my womb, but in a matter of minutes turned off the flat screen on the wall and told us the news. We sat there paralyzed already by fear, but now the truth of it all was quietly and compassionately brought out. "I am sorry, but we are unable to find the baby's heartbeat."

Earlier that morning, at my pre-natal exam, my doctor had mentioned that next time we would hear the baby's heartbeat, and I remembered thinking, "I guess that will be this afternoon." But now I knew that my motherly inclination was right. It was like I had been prepared for this outcome, even though I had never spoken a word of this to my husband, as I didn't want to speak death or be a pessimist. He said he never in a million years expected to hear this news. We were supposed to get our baby's first photos, not this. I am fortunate that it occurred this way rather than as a sudden miscarriage, since the shock would have been so much more intense.

The support we received was amazing. We were referred to the pregnancy loss centre to aid us in our emotional (and my physical) healing. The nurse there was extremely caring, for she had gone through five miscarriages and understood exactly what I was feeling. Her response to my emotions along with her knowledge of how to carry on was remarkable. I realized how crucial and beneficial it can be when you acquire the provision of proper care from both medical staff and family and friends.

Our house was filled with the scent and beauty of fresh flower arrangements combined with cards and encouraging heartfelt e-mails. When my husband and I found out I was pregnant, we decided to tell our close family and friends even though many people wait until after their first ultrasound. We thought if something traumatic was ever to occur we would not go through it alone, and at the same time, we also wanted to share the joy we were experiencing as we waited for our new little one's arrival.

~ ~

My little baby who was forming inside of me is now up in heaven singing with the angels. No longer am I sustaining the tiny one's life, but the Giver of all life is taking care of my angel baby. The journey of grieving has just begun, but the realization of it all has not yet transpired, and a gaping wound surrounds my heart and emotions. My eyes are raw and I feel as if I could not cry anymore, yet I know that God bottles up all my tears. I pray that these tears will be turned into rivers of healing that will flow and touch other people's heart strings.

The disappointment isn't easily relinquished, but Derek and I have been given the ability to move on. We know that the birthing of our dreams for another little one will become reality in God's perfect timing as we look forward to holding another child in our arms. We are so blessed to have our daughter, Hope, and she has been influential in our healing with all her smiles and the joy that she expresses. It astounded us how, at such a young age, she understood all that occurred and had a knowledge that the baby in Mommy's tummy was now in heaven.

I now am starting to comprehend what a woman experiences after she loses her unborn baby. Though you haven't met your child, there is still an innate sense of loss as you try to visualize this tiny one. You pick out names, but will never be able to put a face to the name until you meet your angel baby in heaven.

The design of one's life is fashioned at conception as the chromosomes come together in formation. Then, three weeks later, a new heart begins to beat. I am reminded how the heartbeat of God thumps for each one of us. It is our decision to either accept and connect with His heartbeat or to try and live this life and sustain it on our own. I choose to stay close to God's heartbeat and let His life-giving power flow through me. This power has been evident in seeing me through, and my faith continues to uphold me in every step that I walk on this journey of life.

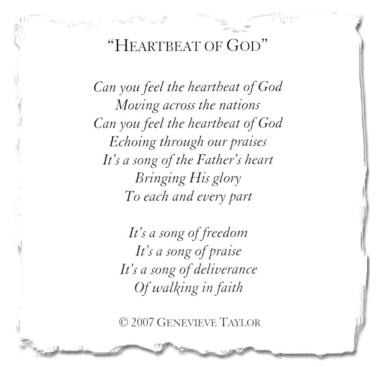

"Heartbeat of God"

Can you feel the heartbeat of God
Moving across the nations
Can you feel the heartbeat of God
Echoing through our praises
It's a song of the Father's heart
Bringing His glory
To each and every part

It's a song of freedom
It's a song of praise
It's a song of deliverance
Of walking in faith

© 2007 Genevieve Taylor

I am not ready to fall asleep…my husband, Derek, and I had a heart-to-heart conversation before he drifted off. "I just can't wait to hear our baby's heartbeat, I just need to hear it. I believe in faith that I will in a few short months, but I want to hear it now."

Yes, we are again expecting another little miracle of life. After losing our unborn child only a few months ago, it makes us a little nervous to start dreaming all over again. We don't want to be let down. So, instead of wandering off into dreamland, I lie awake in my guest room, visualizing how my little one's room will take shape as I think through all the colors and styles of how it will be designed that are floating around in my head—chocolate brown, cream, tan, and pink to finish it off (or baby blue if a little prince comes our way).

For the first time Derek had the opportunity to be a part of the process of taking the home pregnancy test, since the other two times he was out of the country. He read the "+" and was so excited to know that on Canada Day we made our own fireworks, with what looks like a lasting and life-making impression! We were so delighted to look ahead on the calendar to March 23, 2008, and notice that Easter Sunday is when our baby is due. It speaks to us of resurrection and life—yes, life that is truly symbolic and means more to us now than ever. Once again we hold onto hope and know that God surrounds us with His protection and love, just as my womb covers and surrounds this tiny life. The connection of the umbilical cord brings nourishment to this wonder in the making, even as my heart is being linked and has already fallen in love with this little unique soul.

"CONNECTED"

Not whole without Your presence
You only satisfy
Complete, surrounded, protected
My supply
Dressed in Your righteousness
Showcased by grace
Peace, passion and purpose
Kissed by Your face

You are my hopes, You are my dreams
And I'll stay connected to You
You are my source, You are my life
And I'll stay connected to You
You are my joy, You are my sight
And I'll stay connected to You

In everything You are
In everything You were
In everything You'll always be

© 2007 GENEVIEVE TAYLOR

Above All, There is Hope

"MOMMY, I want to put on my dancing tu-tu." It is funny how Hope already associates her bubble-gum-pink dress as her dancing outfit. (She wore it to a wedding where she enjoyed dancing and twirling around the slippery dance floor.)

Standing at her closet door, I bring to mind the time before she was born, when Derek and I transformed what was then our urban chic music room—with a feature wall of chestnut red—into a lilac purple and lime green bedroom with cream organza accents fit for a little princess. That night we organized music books and sheet music to make room for the teddy bears and other treasures essential to complete a palace for a princess. Derek pulled out a copy of "I Hope You Dance,"[8] made popular by Lee Ann Womack. Two years later, it has become such a familiar tune in our home, for Hope so beautifully puts together the phrasing of the song (with a few missed words) with her "Hope" singing bear (given by her great-nana) that moves, sings and

---

[8] Sillers, Tia and Sanders, Mark D. "I Hope You Dance" © 2000 Famous Music Publishing, Leonard. Universal/MCA Music.

so aptly displays the outward expression of the steps we dance throughout our lives.

They say true love stands the test of time. Tonight I watched the movie *A Walk to Remember*[9] with Derek. This great love story evoked my emotions and led me to tears as I recalled how our own love for one another has been strengthened as we walked through this crossing holding onto each other.

"You are a treasure to me
that as far as these eyes could see,
a reflection beyond the soul
to the deepest part that
makes me whole."

These are just a glimpse of the words I wrote to Derek and sang on our wedding day. Every day I am reminded of those words as I look up over the mantle of our fireplace to the portrait taken on that day. The scenery was so picturesque, with the stone archway and banister set so perfectly to create the background with the waterfall flowing out of the rocks and crevices. The reflective camera lens made it appear like we were standing in front of a vast water pond, shimmering with a mirror image. The portrayal of love truly captured the beauty and joy of our love, as well as an understanding that even though you can

---

[9] Di Novi, Denise and Lowry, Hunt (Producers), & Shankman, Adam (Director). (2002). *A Walk to Remember*. United States: Warner Bros. Pictures.

believe in fairytales, it is the walking together in real life's circumstances that will attest to whether or not you will live happily ever after. Now, more than ever, I am thankful for true love, which would otherwise have been shattered if it had been built upon false hopes and pretenses. Our trials show that with perseverance you can walk through any path that may emerge.

Twinkle, twinkle little star... There is one little star out tonight. Even though in the backdrop there are millions upon millions, I can only see one shining against the black onyx sky. In this moment I sit on my deck, alone, but far from feeling alone as I breathe in the crisp fresh air, reflect on my journey so far, and continue to dream. I look up and see the window to my Hope's room where she is sleeping so peacefully. Her sweet voice is recorded in my mind as her version of "Twinkle, Twinkle Little Star" plays in my head and becomes the ambiance music that awakens this romantic surrounding.

This is how God looks at us—like there is only one of us—yet in reality, there are billions of people on the earth and He delights in each one of us as we shine in our own distinct fashion.

I saw Genevieve Taylor the first time I walked into Destiny Christian Centre International. She was leading the music. She was a beautiful, petite ball of energy with an amazing voice. I cried all the way through listening to her sing. It was so beautiful! She was very thin—vivacious is a great word to describe her. Every time I heard her, I knew I wanted to get to know her better. Over time I realized she was getting more and more portly, and I was thrilled to hear she was having a baby.

One event we had at the church for Valentine's Day was for the Women of Destiny, a group of women at our church. I had the opportunity to pray with Genevieve, and as I put my arms around her to give her a hug an overwhelming sense of much pain came over me. I asked her if she was going through something and she said yes. I did not know at that time exactly what was going on with her. Over the next several months, I watched her blossom as she continued leading the music at DCCI. Every time I saw her sing, I marveled at how much she loved God and was able to express it so deeply and profoundly as she sang each week.

I actually saw her the day before her beautiful daughter, Hope, was born. She looked wonderful, as always, in a cute maternity outfit, simply glowing as she waited to have her child. I did not know that this was a prelude to one of the darkest times of her life.

I did not hear what was going on with her immediately. I just know that the next time I saw her she was a mere shell of the beautiful lady I had been watching and admiring. I'd heard that she was suffering from extreme depression after having had the baby. Having dealt with postpartum myself when I had my second child, I was extremely empathetic. I knew what it was like to have walked down the very dark tunnel of depression. I could relate, and I knew that prayer was the only answer that would really help her. I had walked several months of very deep and dark *depression until I had finally given my life back to the Lord after years of not walking with Him. Anti-depressants had sent me further into depression, and it was clearly one of the worst and darkest times of my life.*

As I saw her, I had some feeling of what she was going through. I remembered how I had sobbed for her in February and knew that this *was what I had gotten a revelation of. Genevieve had gone from being the beautiful, vivacious singer to a vacant shell of a woman. She would look right at you, but you knew she wasn't really there. It seemed like she was moving in slow motion. She barely smiled, whereas in the past, the stage lights were only mere reflections from her smile whenever she sang. You always knew she had spent a lot of time with God before she sang, and her face always glowed as a result. Now this glow was nowhere to be seen.*

As a church we prayed for Genevieve and her family regularly. There were many times she would come to mind and I would pray for her every time. I seemed to really feel her pain. Maybe it was my own memories that I could look at, now years later, with different eyes. I can't really explain why, except I knew that I needed to pray for her whenever prompted to do so. One time I had an opportunity to speak to her after church. I felt an overwhelming need to pray for her and I asked her if I could pray for her. She looked at me with those dim eyes and said "I don't know…" in a flat voice.

The normal melodious voice was now toneless. It was so sad! I was not offended, though, since I could understand where she was at that point. She barely knew or even remembered me. I said, *"That's okay. I can pray for you anyway later."*

Over time, I watched this lovely lady walk out of where she had been. The beautiful lady with the amazing voice was back. Now there was a deeper strength, a quality about her that had not been there before. A sense of maturity and a deep love of God showed through her music and every time she prayed out loud. The beautiful smile when she sang was back!

In April of this year, I had the opportunity to go to Winnipeg with our Pastor and the team from DCCI, including Genevieve. She, TJ and I were the only women in what was mostly a group of guys, so we would sit together frequently whenever we ate. Once again I marveled at her angelic voice as she sang during the services. Having a musical background, I have a deep appreciation of good music and singing. There are notes that she hits that are nothing short of amazing, and when one song in particular was done, despite the small crowd in attendance, you could believe there was an angelic choir present, the sound of the voices was so strong.

Genevieve was pregnant and glowing again. She ate like there was no tomorrow. We would eat late at night after the services. She could polish off a huge meal for someone so small. She was her beautiful, bubbly self. It was great to see her smile.

We had made arrangements to meet one afternoon for coffee. Genevieve said they were having an ultrasound and that they would meet with me later that afternoon. I got a call saying it had to be a little later, but we finally met. Genevieve walked in and I knew immediately *something was wrong. She said the baby did not have a heartbeat. Right away we prayed together. This time I could be there to help support her. My own son and daughter-in-law had lost three babies in the early stages, so again I could relate to where she was at. This time, though, was different. Yes, there was sadness, and yes, there was loss, but this time an inner God–given strength was shining through.*

Praise God, they knew that I was in their lives to help them get through this. I am so thankful for the ministry that God has brought me to. I am so thankful for getting to know a beautiful lady like Genevieve. Thankful to be a small part in helping her achieve the God–given dreams that she has to complete this book and record her CD. Thankful to see her accomplish a dream to impact and change many people's lives. What the enemy has meant for harm, God has turned around into something very, very good.

~Melody

Rose-Colored Glasses

IT'S FUNNY HOW it is so easy to relate to simple little children's stories, which is what happened to me with the story of the little fish in *Finding Nemo*.[10] I'm especially drawn to the scene at the beginning when Nemo's mom and dad are getting ready for their new arrivals. They go and check on the hundreds of little fish eggs and are overcome with a smile of anticipation for their soon-to-be path of parenthood as they watch their little ones dream.

In much the same way, my parents had great anticipation for my life. My mom once gave me a little card that I still hold on to and treasure: "Hoping your life will always be full of sweet dreams." My dad has a gift of writing little notes and poems. I recall a number of occasions when he wrote me a little note and said, "I can't wait to hear the solo you are working on." After he arrived home from work, I would get out my white Sony ghetto blaster and stand in front of the fireplace and sing my little heart out, which would always bring tears to the audience of my

---

[10] Walters, Graham (Producer), & Stanton, Andrew. (2003). *Finding Nemo*. United States: Walt Disney Pictures/Pixar Animation Studios.

dad's eyes. My parents were always cheering me on—I knew I was cherished, treasured, accepted, valued and important when I looked into their eyes.

When I look into Hope's eyes I see Derek. She has her daddy's blue eyes and amazing long dark eyelashes. Hope has been blessed with an amazing father and I'm so proud of how he carried her through those first weeks and months when I wasn't able to! My struggle, however, was to find the confidence that I would be visible in Hope's eyes as well and that I would be the mother she would need and love and be proud of. I felt like a failure in my own eyes, and knew that I was battling against the pressures of what I perceived were people's expectations of me—both of those who believed I could do it and those who didn't—as well as the remorse for not having been there for Hope when she was first starting out her life in this world.

At Hope's baby dedication I sang "In My Daughter's Eyes" as a duet with my friend who had just delivered her daughter, Faith. We thought it would be special to have our daughters Faith and Hope dedicated together.

"IN MY DAUGHTER'S EYES"
by James Slater (performed by Martina McBride)

In my daughter's eyes
I am a hero
I am strong and wise and I know no fear
But the truth is plain to see
She was sent to rescue me

I see who I want to be
In my daughter's eyes

In my daughter's eyes
Everyone is equal
Darkness turns to light
And the world is at peace
This miracle God gave to me
Gives me strength when I am weak
I find reason to believe
In my daughter's eyes

When she wraps her hand around my finger
Oh, it puts a smile in my heart
Everything becomes a little clearer
I realize what love is all about

It's hangin' on when your heart has had enough
It's giving more when you feel like giving up
I've seen the light
It's in my daughter's eyes

In my daughter's eyes
I can see the future
A reflection of who I am and what will be
Though she'll grow and someday leave
Maybe raise a family
When I'm gone I hope you'll see
How happy she made me
For I'll be there...
In my daughter's eyes[11]

---

[11] Slater, James. "In My Daughter's Eyes" © 2003 Cherry Lane Music Co.
(performed by Martina McBride) All rights reserved. Used by
permission.

At that time, I felt like I was nothing in my daughter's eyes, and I thought everyone else felt the same way about me. *Am I a good mom? How do people perceive me as a mother?* My friend so nicely gave me the choice of verses to sing, as I had explained to her that I was unable to sing the first few lines of the first verse. I have always meant the words that I sing, and at that time I didn't think I could say that I was a hero and strong and wise with no fear. I was still broken and in the process of needing healing and restoration.

After Hope's birth, it was like I had vanished—swallowed up by the big "shark" of postpartum psychosis—but one day I was let out, like Jonah came out from the belly of a whale. Just like Nemo's daddy held on to Nemo, whispering, "Daddy's here," so my husband Derek held onto his tiny new little daughter and assured her "Daddy's here," in a tone that oozed out compassion and love mingled with the unsure feeling of how he was going to make it through. *Will my wife ever return to us?* I marvel at how he would ensure Hope would see me every day in the psychiatric ward at the hospital so I could still somehow bond with my baby even though I looked so vacant, as many have described in these pages already.

After I started to heal, I knew that, with great purpose and determination, I needed to tell my story in a transparent way, allowing others to see through my heart and emotions. I have always been one who likes to cover things up and look perfect, especially when it comes to what I wear. As I write this book and begin to share my story, I feel naked, yet I know I am clothed with grace.

As I gaze into the sky and marvel at the multicolored facets of a rainbow all mingled together, I see a reflection of God's heart and passion to see people coming together, each dressed in their own color and shining in their moment. I love how God wrapped the promise of His grace in the extravagant beauty of color!

I will always carry a picture in my mind of my little Hope in her bubble-gum-pink dress—she has been the very color of hope to me. Meanwhile, here I stand in my usual black and white (accessorized with silver and clear transparent jewelry), but today I hold a hand out to the different colors that surround me. You see, when I go shopping, I look around and say, "That color reminds me of…" a particular person or, "I could totally see that outfit on someone." Everyone has their own sense and style of fashion, and in the same way, everyone should be encouraged to play out their own style and song, just as I have learned to just be me. The picture of Hope in her pink dress reminds me of the other people whose "colors" have covered, enriched and energized my life as they chose to shine in their moments with me.

If I were to try to create a shining moment, I wouldn't stand before you and make a pie, cater a meal or arrange numbers like my accountant. I would stand before you and sing from my heart a song of passion, a song of hope, a song to capture the moment. There is a song for every moment—even as I look down at my watch and see the hands counting off each second—and I have realized that when you wake up and discover your passion and really do it, then you are truly living.

For all of you who have surrounded me with your many colors just like Joseph was covered in his coat of many colors, it is now that I say my thanks and take these moments to describe the beauty of it all. You have been a glimmer of light in a dark time, a song of joy in times of rejoicing (a picture of what I see when I read the third chapter of Ecclesiastes).

Even though it means being vulnerable, I'm choosing to shine in the "Now Moments" that God grants as I share my experiences and allow Him to use my life and story and song to declare His glory and bring the color of His grace to those lives I encounter. I am amazed as people continue to join with me and display their colors in this time as well. Writing this book and recording my CD are just two examples of moments when we all shine so much more brilliantly together!

ॐ ◌

I think back to the first week after Hope was born. That summer, the rain barreled down in buckets as the overflow spilled out of the ponds and onto the pathway behind our home. As I held my new baby nestled in my arms, I watched the new mother goose protecting and taking care of her newest arrivals.

"You can either sink or swim—if the path is flooded, then get into the lifeboat or swim to safety!"

Two years later, Hope and I enjoy taking our walks together down the same paths. We are almost home and she starts running.

"Slow down, be careful," I insist. "Oh no!" I run to pick her up and kiss her scraped little knees.

"Mommy you need to carry me."

The rest of the way I hold her cradled in my arms until we arrive safely at home. There are times where we, too, need to be carried, held in a long embrace where words are absent, but love so intense is communicated nonetheless.

"PURE"[12]
by Kari Jobe

Your love is pure, Your love is precious
Your love is all I need
Your love surrounds me, Your love astounds me
Your love is everything
I run to You when my heart is weak
I cling to You, You're all I seek
It's my heart's desire to be close to You
Here in Your arms I'll find my strength

Everything I want, everything I hope in
Everything my heart cries out for
Everything I want, everything I hope in
Everything my heart cries out for

---

[12] Jobe, Kari. "Pure" © 2003 Kari Jobe/Gateway Create Publishing / Integrity's Praise! Music. Used by permission. Please visit Kari Jobe's website: www.karijobe.com

I am thankful that God can turn things around and that lives can be touched and transformed. You might never fully know or realize what your word of encouragement might do for someone. I am reminded how the writers of the worship songs so powerfully orchestrated the music that brought me hope, healing and restoration. Though they never met me, their songs were used to touch my mind and awaken my spirit to soar above the situation and take hold of life.

"BURST"

Speak to situations
Learn to overcome
Moving of mountains
When we call on the One
Mighty name of Jesus
Power to unfold
We see breakthrough now explode

Something's about to burst
Something's about to change
Turnaround is coming, in Jesus' name

No weapon that's formed
Will slow you down
For God will turn it around
He'll take your limitations
That hold
Propel you forward
To your dreams

© 2007 GENEVIEVE TAYLOR

I still remember the times when my friends or family would write notes of encouragement or take the time to sit with me over a piece of lemon meringue pie in the hospital cafeteria. I may have been talking nonsense, but they still held onto the hope that I would rediscover myself and come around and be all that God had planned me to be. It was like I was stripped of everything. I realize now what it is like to die to your own selfish ambitions and pride.

When I was ill I would be so discouraged that, instead of writing words of life, I would put myself down. After I started to heal, I discovered notes I had written in notebooks as well as one on the back of a picture frame in my living room. They were words twisted so far from the truth, lies that I wasn't any good. It is funny how the enemy of our souls tried to use the very things that I loved to do to bring discouragement and hopelessness, as I expressed in my writing. I recall numerous times where my husband would take what I had written and sow seeds of life and point me back to the truth, the truth that would set me free. John 8:32 reads, "Then you will know the truth, and the truth will set you free."

Below is a poem my Dad wrote in his own unique way of expressing his feelings and capturing the moment.

I woke up one day
I'm sad to say
My daughter had gone away
Thoughts rambled on and on

Her safe full life was gone
Not thinking straight
Thought she lost her mate
With trouble trying to relate
Confused and sedate
Totally changed life
Filled with strife
Reality cut like a knife
We wanted to bawl
But we stood straight and tall
For we knew our God changes all
Speaking Shalom
Would soon bring her home
Not with a mind on roam
So you know God is great
He never shows up late
Our Genevieve can now relate
We knew it would take time
For things to realign
A touch from our Divine
Was the one thing on our mind
Thankful to God this day
Our Genevieve was OK
No more dreaming in a day
Of thoughts gone astray
Her bubbly array
Is now back to stay

~Love, your Dad

THROUGH IT ALL
A Mother's Love

IT IS APPARENT that, no matter what you encounter in becoming a mother, one thing is certain—the end result outweighs what you are experiencing. Whether it is the heartache and disappointment you bear month after month while trying to conceive, or losing your baby before you go to term or the postpartum depression that you might go through after the arrival, it is evident that whatever you walk through is worth it all when you look into the eyes of your child and hold them in your arms as they clasp their little arms around your neck.

You can't always prepare for everything, but you can continue to accept life as it comes and learn with great determination to stand strong when the unexpected is at your door. "What to Expect When You're Expecting" isn't really fair to say, for you can't always see what lies ahead. What you *can* do, however, is keep the faith and hold onto the hope deep within you that something good can transpire out of the difficult situations we all face.

I am so delighted to be a mom. Oh sure, I dreamed of climbing the corporate ladder or becoming a superstar, and I could have put motherhood on the back burner. But I look back now and ponder all that I have become, and while I continue to learn what it takes, I realize that I am growing and changing just as quickly as my little one. There is nothing else like a mother's love, and I am blessed to have known and experienced this. What an honor, to give all my heart and attention to my child!

℠ ℗

Following one of my appointments with my doctor about a year and a half after being in the hospital, I was forced to take a different route out of the hospital because the one door was being replaced with a new one. With butterflies in my stomach, I walked through the hallway and was led towards Unit 49. On my way I passed by the treatment and recovery room for ECT. I peeked into the window of the locked doors to the unit. For a moment I summoned up as much as I could remember of the time I spent there. As I turned around and moved toward the outside door, with my beautiful daughter clenching my hand, I realized how thankful I am for what I have and how proud I am to have walked through that dark and clouded point in time. I am grateful to hold onto "My Little Hope" as I become stronger and to know the promise that all things really do work out for our good. God opens new doors when others shut, and I am amazed as I see how God is continuing to open new doors and opportunities to visit places far beyond what I ever dreamed I would ever see firsthand.

I am a success story, and it saddens my heart when I hear of the outcomes of some postpartum psychosis stories, where suicide seems the only way out of the black hole that swallows up futures and lives. Even though my case was very extreme, I believe God totally protected me, for I never wanted to take my life. Sure, at the time it was like my life was taken from me, as it wasn't really me—it was like I had died but I was still living. I don't take life for granted, but cherish every waking moment. I am truly living, and the one who breathes His breath of life within freed my soul. The one night in Unit 49 when I was "recording" and "debuting" my imaginary record, I sang one of my favorite songs, which throughout that time my family on occasion would sing along with me while in the hospital. "This Is Life" has become an anthem my heart, mind and soul echoes as I realize the healing power it brought me.

"THIS IS LIFE"[13]
by Laura Woodley

Eyes can't see the way You hold me
Or how I'm hidden in Your heart
Minds don't know all that You've told me
Or how I ache for where You are
It's invisible to the world
Incredible to the angels

Not since Eden have they seen this sight
Everlasting life

You are all over
You are around
You are inside
This is life, this is life

Come in empty and I leave filled
Bring my sickness and I leave healed
Brokenhearted, You mend every piece
Come in captive and I leave free

Through it all, I never for a second lost my ability to worship, and I believe my praise brought me through. I consider it an honor to lead people into the presence of God and capture the "now moments of worship." You can be singing the same song, but capture a unique flavor in that instant where God's presence, His sustaining power and His peace overtake you. You can't recreate that moment, so live in the "now" and take it all in.

There may be times when you feel as if you have nothing left within you and you are unsure what will be written on the next page. The song seems to fade and the chaos of life seems to overwhelm you, and you feel as if you are never going to make it through another day, let alone see your dreams fulfilled. Then, somehow, in the depths you begin to hear a melody arise and strength starts to flow and set you in motion toward a higher plain where you view things with new eyesight. Sometimes our vision becomes clouded or blurred, but with the proper spectacles everything can be in alignment.

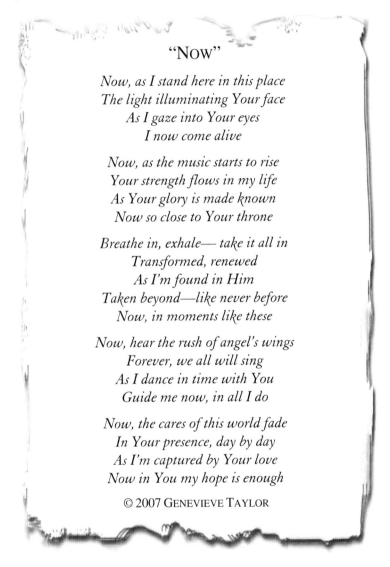

"Now"

Now, as I stand here in this place
The light illuminating Your face
As I gaze into Your eyes
I now come alive

Now, as the music starts to rise
Your strength flows in my life
As Your glory is made known
Now so close to Your throne

Breathe in, exhale— take it all in
Transformed, renewed
As I'm found in Him
Taken beyond—like never before
Now, in moments like these

Now, hear the rush of angel's wings
Forever, we all will sing
As I dance in time with You
Guide me now, in all I do

Now, the cares of this world fade
In Your presence, day by day
As I'm captured by Your love
Now in You my hope is enough

© 2007 Genevieve Taylor

Medication, therapy and a support system helped me obtain clear vision when coupled with the undeniable power of God's healing that made me whole. When my own song wasn't enough to preserve me, I would hold onto other people's songs of encouragement that I am sure helped them and so many others carry on as well.

"TRUST HIS HEART"[14]
by Babbie Mason and Eddie Carswell

All things work for our good
Though sometimes we can't see how they could
Struggles that break our hearts in two
Sometimes blind us to the truth

Our Father knows what's best for us
His ways are not our own
So when your pathway grows dim,
And you just can't see Him
Remember you're never alone

God is too wise to be mistaken
God is too good to be unkind
So when you don't understand
When you don't see His plan
When you can't trace His hand
Trust His heart

He sees the master plan
And He holds our future in His hands
So don't live as those who have no hope
All our hope is found in Him

We see the present clearly
But He sees the first and the last
And like a tapestry He's weaving you and me
To someday be just like Him

He alone is faithful and true
He alone knows what is best for you
So when you don't understand
When you don't see His plan
When you can't trace His hand
Trust His heart

Children love to make up little stories. I love listening to Hope read her version of a narrative as she interprets the pictures and conveys the story in her own words. She closes her storybook with, "The End." This book is nearing the end, but it is merely just the beginning of the story that continues to be written on the path of hope. Our steps are enlightened along the way as we learn to trust and keep in time with God's heart. Each beat gives us momentum, just like the moving hand on the face of a watch propels forward from second to second.

As I write to you today I'm looking back, yet moving ahead. I'm taking hold of promises my heavenly Father whispered, though they seemed so far away. I don't want to go back and relive the pain and the confusion, the fear of not being good enough or trying to obtain perfection. I know that there is no condemnation and that I don't need to be perfect. I just live every day holding onto the hope that lives within and carries me through. It is not just a coincidence that my daughter's name is Hope.

Strangely enough, at the time when I was sick and my mind was confused, I told my husband to change my daughter's name. My thoughts were so twisted that, for some reason, I wanted to live without "Hope." She has a unique purpose and destiny, and already in her life she has lived out her name by giving her mom hope when it seemed like all hope was gone. I would hold her in my arms and stare into space like she wasn't really there, but all the while she was restoring my purpose to live and eventually escape the bubble that surrounded me so that I could "enjoy the moments" that life would bring.

After I became well I feared that the bond between Hope and I was severed, and that she would only be Daddy's little girl because of the time I felt I missed during the first few months of her life. I can say now without a doubt that all fear has been removed, and I share a very close relationship like no one else with my little angel. I treasure every second that I am with her, for she captivates her mommy's heart.

"Hope, do you know Mommy loves you?"

"I know, Mommy", she replies with her sweet voice. That is all I need to hear, and the song begins to play…

It's gonna be worth it,
It's gonna be worth it,
It's gonna be worth it all

Yes, it is worth it…..through it all[15]

---

[15] Springer, Rita. "Worth It All" © 2002 Rita Springer/River Oaks Music Company (a div. of EMI Christian Music Publishing). All rights reserved. Used by permission.

But You, God

"But You, God, but You, God, but You…"

THE MELODY FOR THE CHORUS rose up effortlessly and began to become a little tune I enjoyed singing. The words were so simple, yet they held a deeper meaning. It was the last song that I wrote for the worship CD project, and it seemed especially fitting as I marveled at how it all came together.

I remember bringing the simple phrase and melody into the studio to begin working on it. I wanted to create an arrangement for the live CD recording and presented the melody for the chorus even though it was yet to be completed. It was so neat to take the power behind the melody and watch the bridge develop, but still there were no verses.

We decided to leave it until the next week and believed that it would come. The following week, I started to receive excerpts from the family members and friends that I had asked to help tell my story in light of my memory loss. These letters were difficult to read, and even though I was now walking whole and healed, I knew it was time to face the reality of the state of mind I had been in and truly say, "This is what could have been, but You, God."

The prognosis for my condition was that I most likely would develop a bi-polar disorder that would need to be maintained by medication to sustain a normal life. It was suggested that we do not have any other children, for there is a high chance of a re-occurrence of postpartum psychosis. I am amazed to see how things were turned around and that my destiny and my children's destinies will be fulfilled. You see, my dreams never changed, but the path and the circumstances to get there sure took us for a ride.

An hour before I had to go back into the studio to work on the unfinished song, I sat in my sister's guest room scrambling to finish the lyrics, and what you'll read below is what transpired. At that moment the words "I don't understand who I am" didn't seem to make sense, but after I met with my mom and she gave me her copy of the excerpt she wrote for the book, it confirmed why these words were so perfect.

At my lowest point I couldn't remember if I was "Gen, Genevieve, or Geni," but now I know who I am in Christ—He never forgot my name, and now I will live to tell how He rewrites what could have been into what will be. He always keeps His promises, and what could have been a blues riff or a sad country song turned into a powerful praise tune overflowing with hope.

"BUT YOU, GOD"

I don't understand
Who I am
The reflection you see
No part of me
Promises remembered
Hope renewed
Rediscovering purpose
You rewrite, You undo

But You God, but You God, but You
But You God, but You God, but You

I now understand
Who I am
The reflection you see
You mirrored in me
Promises remembered
Hope renewed
Rediscovering purpose
You rewrite, You undo

Astounding, amazing
Miraculous, truth
Glorious, unchanging
Shining through

© 2007 GENEVIEVE TAYLOR

Thank You!

"ON MY OWN,"[16] the name of a song from the musical *Les Miserables*, stirs something inside me as I recognize how grateful I am that I am not alone.

My whole persona has definitely been shaken as I realize the benefits not only to myself, but also to the people around me as they have been allowed to use their own distinct talents and desires to lend a hand in something they may never have even touched in their life. It has been amazing to watch the display as the pieces of the puzzle have all connected to make one beautiful masterpiece. Everyone's song has come together—someone singing alto, another tenor and who could forget the bass!—as the melody is heard so much more beautifully then it would have been on its own.

The essential parts and pieces are especially apparent in Hope's little life, and I am so thankful for all the love, care and attention she received and

---

[16] Boublil, Alain; Caird, John; Kretzmer, Herbert; Natel, Jean-Marc; Nunn, Trevor and Schönberg, Claude-Michel, in *Les Miserables* by Alain Boublil and Claude-Michel Schönberg "On My Own" Music and Lyrics © 1986 by Alain Boublil Music Ltd. (ASCAP) Mechanical and Publication Rights for the USA Administered by Alain Boublil Music Ltd. (ASCAP) C/O Stephen Tenenbaum & Co. Inc. 1775 Broadway, Suite 708, New York, NY 10019. International Copyright Secured. All Rights Reserved.

continues to acquire. After Hope was born, while I was in the hospital there was no way for my husband, Derek, to keep a full time job as well as be Mr. Mom. I am thankful for our close family and friends who assisted him with the "motherly" duties—the midnight feedings, diaper changes and finding a new art to burping—all performed without missing any of the nurturing aspects of love and affection that at the time I was unable to fully give.

As I watch Hope so carefully nurture her own baby doll, feed her, burp her, change her diaper, take her for walks in her little stroller and show her affection, a smile comes over me and I know she was well taken care of during my absent-mindedness. She loves babies and delights in any opportunity to hold and see a little one. This chapter is my way of communicating my appreciation to all of you who ensured these pieces of the puzzle were in place for the foundation of my daughter's life to be built. You may never fully know how you touched someone's life in what might have seemed small or insignificant, but in the grand scheme of life it was a bridge that helped me over the waters that tried to swallow up my life.

God, my memory is filled with snapshots and impressions—lasting monuments in my heart clearly displaying Your faithfulness as I held onto Your promises. Through it all, I give You all the glory.

Derek, you certainly are my rock; my dreams have come true with you as my Prince. I know you will tease me for using the love lingo. You are a man of integrity and mean what you say, and my words cannot outshine all that you do for me. I can see why God chose you for me and it becomes even more evident as time goes by. Thank you for believing in me and allowing me to pursue my dreams. "I love you with my whole heart and I will never let you go."

Hope Anastella, your name just says it all…you are full of grace and you are my little star. I cherish all the mommy and daughter moments we share together. It touches my heart when I hear you sing, laugh, dance and smile. "There's no hole in my heart, you filled up that part."

To my angel baby and to my baby-to-be, you will always hold a special place in mommy's heart.

Mom and Dad, you have always fueled my heart's passion and taught me that dreams really can come true—and that marriage and commitment outweigh any hardship. Mom, you probably never thought that giving me a "Mother's Journal" would help me to begin to pen my story. Dad, your rhymes have been influential, and I do get my poetic side from you (not my singing). I now understand when you say, "We love you, princess, with every piece of our hearts and in the same way you love your daughter Hope."

To my brother Chris, my sister, Elisa, and my brother Tom: it is so neat to see the closeness and connection between us becoming stronger as we see all our childhood dreams become reality. It is an honor to have you all taking part in the book and CD projects and to see us "kids" coming together to do what we were made to do.

To my parents-in-law, Bob and Brenda, and my brothers-in-law, Gene and Trent: your love and support means so much. Brenda, we especially appreciate all you were able to provide when we needed you. Hugs to you all.

Dr. Petrov and the staff of Unit 49: I acknowledge your dedication and ambition as being a part of my recovery.

Caryn, here's to our stay at Unit 49, a.k.a. "The Spa." What appeared to be a detour has emerged into an understanding that God can turn things around, and now we have acquired an amazing friendship!

Tobie, I remember that beautiful summer day at a family picnic where you said, "You need to write a book about your journey." You sparked the passion and infused something deep within me to create this book.

Steena, as you gave me a signed copy of your book, *Once Upon A Dream*, you awakened and encouraged me in my own writing. I appreciate the time you took to arrange the excerpts and assemble the text to submit to the publishers. Thanks for sharing this encouraging word with me, as it has also become one close to my heart: "Through your everything, I pray hope will be your guide."

Kari and Tom, remember the little journal you gave me while I was in the hospital? Inside it read, "May this book help you rediscover who you are…May it be filled with words of joy, love, deep thoughts, challenges and growth…Know always that you are loved and that God has His hand on your life and He will guide you through all things—even this…Your latter will be greater than the past." Kari, thank you for using your gift of writing to pen my Bio for the website.

While leading worship one Sunday morning, a spontaneous song arose: "When I don't know what to do, I will worship You." Thank you to Pastors Greg and Heather Gill and the members of DCCI for your prayers and for believing that my destiny will be fulfilled.

My story could never have been completed without all of you who walked alongside me and who wrote segments for the book. I appreciate your honesty about the situation I faced.

To all of you along my journey, thank you for your encouragement and for being your piece to the puzzle. To those who helped shape who I am and gave me the opportunity to develop my voice and sing, I am truly blessed. I am amazed to see the connections in making dreams become reality.

Word Alive Press, thank you for bringing this book to life. Caroline, I am so pleased with the support I have received and I marvel as it has developed. Larissa, the countless hours you spent in editing and page layout to ensure every detail is precise and sealed with excellence is remarkable.

Rosie Moyer, you truly capture the moment through the eyes of your camera lens, and I am delighted to work with you on these projects.

To the writers of the songs referred to within this book…you have been an inspiration.

"THROUGH IT ALL"

Chaos of life overwhelms me
Lost to the unknown
Shattered heart needing healing
Found in You alone

We will rise and we will fall
Yet we will make it through it all
Stepping forward, not alone
We will move on
We worship You, we worship You
We worship You
As we're going through

You alone prove faithful
On this journey of time
Surround, sustain me in Your presence
The giver of all life

Stepping forward, moving on
Sounding heaven's song

© 2007 GENEVIEVE TAYLOR

THROUGH IT ALL
Song References

Boublil, Alain; Caird, John; Kretzmer, Herbert; Natel, Jean-Marc; Nunn, Trevor and Schönberg, Claude-Michel in *Les Miserables* by Alain Boublil and Claude-Michel Schönberg. "On My Own" Music and Lyrics © 1986 by Alain Boublil Music Ltd. (ASCAP) Mechanical and Publication Rights for the USA Administered by Alain Boublil Music Ltd. (ASCAP) C/O Stephen Tenenbaum & Co. Inc. 1775 Broadway, Suite 708, New York, NY 10019. International Copyright Secured. All Rights Reserved.

Houghton, Israel and Lindsay, Aaron. "I Am Not Forgotten" © 2005 Integrity's Praise! Music, Sound Of The New Breed, Aaron Lindsey Publishing.

Jobe, Kari. "Pure" © 2003 Kari Jobe/Gateway Create Publishing/Integrity's Praise! Music. All rights reserved. Used by permission. Please visit Kari Jobe's website: www.karijobe.com.

Keller, Sherilyn. "So In Need" © 2003 Mercy/Vineyard Publishing (Admin. by Music Services). All rights reserved. Used by permission.

Mason, Babbie and Carswell, Eddie, "Trust His Heart" © 1989 Dayspring Music, LLC (a div. of Word Music Group, Inc.) / May Sun Music (Admin. by Word Music Group, Inc.) / Word Music, LLC (a div. of Word Music Group, Inc.) / Causing Change Music (Admin. by Word Music Group, Inc.). All rights reserved. Used by permission.

Noblitt, Kim. "If You Could See Me Now" © 1992 Hold Onto Music (Admin. by Integrity's! Praise Music)/ Integrity's Praise! Music.

Sillers, Tia and Sanders, Mark D. "I Hope You Dance" © 2000 Famous Music Publishing, Leonard. Universal / MCA Music.

Slater, James, (performed by Martina McBride). "In My Daughter's Eyes" © 2003 Cherry Lane Music Co. All rights reserved. Used by permission.

Smith, Martin; Bronleewe, Matthew Ryan and Smith, Michael W. "Healing Rain" ©2004 Curious? Music UK (Admin. by EMI Christian Music Publishing) Word Music, LLC (a div. of Word Music Group, Inc.) Smittyfly Music (Admin. by Word Music Group, Inc.) Songs From The Farm Windswept Pacific Music Ltd.

Springer, Rita. "Worth It All" © 2002 Rita Springer/River Oaks Music Company (a div. of EMI Christian Music Publishing). All rights reserved. Used by permission.

Woodley, Laura. "This is Life" © 2002 Laura Woodley. All rights reserved. International copyright secured. CCLI song #4385761. Used by permission.

WWW.GENEVIEVETAYLOR.CA